The Law Commission
(LAW COM No 314)

INTOXICATION AND CRIMINAL LIABILITY

Presented to the Parliament of the United Kingdom by the Lord Chancellor and Secretary of State for Justice by Command of Her Majesty
January 2009

Cm 7526   £26.60

THE LAW COMMISSION

The Law Commission was set up by the Law Commissions Act 1965 for the purpose of promoting the reform of the law.

The Law Commissioners are:

> The Right Honourable Lord Justice Etherton, *Chairman*
> Professor Elizabeth Cooke
> Mr David Hertzell
> Professor Jeremy Horder
> Mr Kenneth Parker QC

The Chief Executive of the Law Commission is Mr William Arnold.

The Law Commission is located at Steel House, 11 Tothill Street, London SW1H 9LJ.

The terms of this report were agreed on 4 December 2008.

The text of this report is available on the Internet at:

http://www.lawcom.gov.uk/intoxication.htm

THE LAW COMMISSION

INTOXICATION AND CRIMINAL LIABILITY

CONTENTS

THE LAW COMMISSION

INTOXICATION AND CRIMINAL LIABILITY

To the Right Honourable Jack Straw MP, Lord Chancellor and Secretary of State for Justice

PART 1
THE SCOPE OF THIS REPORT

INTRODUCTION

1.1 Many crimes, particularly crimes of violence, are committed when the offender is in a state of extreme or partial intoxication, usually as a result of the voluntary consumption of alcohol but often because of his or her use of (other) drugs, or a combination of alcohol and drugs.[1] This view is supported by a number of empirical studies; for example:

   (1) the Home Office's Statistical Bulletin *Crime in England and Wales 2006/2007*, relying on the 2006/2007 British Crime Survey, states that "there were 1,087,000 violent incidents [in 2006/2007] where the victim believed the offender or offenders to be under the influence of alcohol";[2]

   (2) the same Bulletin, relying again on the 2006/2007 British Crime Survey, suggests that victims believe their offender(s) to be under the influence of alcohol in almost half of violent incidents[3] and under the influence of other drugs in about a fifth of cases;[4] and

   (3) according to the former Prime Minister's 2004 Strategy Unit Report, *Alcohol Harm Reduction Strategy for England*:[5]

      (a) a third of victims of domestic violence say that their assailant had been drinking beforehand;[6]

      (b) heavy drinking raises the risk of a sexual assault being committed;[7]

---

[1] It is to be noted that the law draws no distinction between the effects of (dangerous) drugs voluntarily taken by D and self-inflicted drunkenness; see, eg, *Lipman* [1970] 1 QB 152, 156 and s 6(6) of the Public Order Act 1986.

[2] Page 65.

[3] Above. According to the 2006/2007 British Crime Survey, p 65, the figure is 46%, approximately the same as the figure recorded for 2005/2006 (45%). *Crime in England and Wales 2001/2002: Supplementary Volume* (2003) p 58 records the figure as 47% for that period.

[4] Above, pp 65 and 72 (table 3.06). The figure for 2006/2007 is 17%, compared with 23% for 2005/2006. The figure for 2001/2002 was 21% (*Crime in England and Wales 2001/2002: Supplementary Volume* (2003) p 58).

[5] Cabinet Office, 15 March 2004.

[6] Above, pp 4 and 13.

[7] Above, pp 14 and 46.

(c)   more than half of those arrested for breach of the peace and nearly half of those arrested for causing criminal damage had been drinking;[8] and

(d)   the annual cost of alcohol-related crime and antisocial conduct is about £7.3 billion.[9]

1.2   It follows that the availability (or non-availability) of defences to criminal liability based on intoxication is not just a matter of legal principle. It may have a far-reaching effect on the perception – particularly the perception of a victim and his or her family – of whether justice has been done.[10]

1.3   When we say "intoxication" we are primarily referring to voluntary or "self-induced" intoxication, where the alleged offender ("D") is affected by the voluntary consumption of alcohol or some other drug.

1.4   The issue of *involuntary* intoxication arises where D commits a crime when he or she has been affected by a drug through no (or no significant) fault of his or her own, as when D's food or drink has been surreptitiously "laced" by a third party, or D has been forced to take a drug against his or her will.[11] This is a much less important concern in practice. However, there is still uncertainty over the demarcation between the concepts of voluntary and involuntary intoxication.

1.5   In this Report, we address the issue of intoxication from alcohol or other drugs and its bearing on the criminal liability, if any, of a person charged with an offence, whether it is alleged that D perpetrated the offence or that D took a secondary role in the commission of the offence by assisting or encouraging a perpetrator.[12] We focus, in particular, on the extent to which voluntary intoxication should be available to support a "defence" based on the absence of fault.

---

[8]   Above, p 45.

[9]   Above, pp 13 and 44. For media perceptions, see, eg: *BBC News*, 7 November 2005 "Campaign cuts drink-fuelled crime" http://news.bbc.co.uk/1/hi/england/tyne/4413698.stm; *BBC News*, 27 January 2005 "Alcohol blamed for violent crime" http://news.bbc.co.uk/1/hi/england/london/4212681.stm; *The Sunday Times*, 14 March 2004, p 1: "Drunken street violence out of control, admits government"; and *Evening Standard*, 15 March 2004, p 25: "Binge drinking war as big death toll emerges". In his foreword to the report *Alcohol Harm Reduction Strategy for England*, the then Prime Minister himself stated that "increasingly, alcohol misuse by a small minority is causing ... crime and antisocial behaviour in town and city centres".

[10]   According to the report *Alcohol Harm Reduction Strategy for England*, at pp 4 and 13, 61% of the population consider alcohol-related violence to be worsening.

[11]   It should be noted that D's voluntary consumption of an alcoholic drink which is stronger than D believes it to be does not amount to involuntary intoxication; see *Allen* [1988] *Criminal Law Review* 698.

[12]   The doctrine of secondary liability permits D to be liable to the same extent as a perpetrator (P) for P's offence if D, acting with the state of mind required for secondary liability, encouraged or assisted P to commit that offence. It is also possible, in some circumstances, for D to be liable for P's offence on the basis that D "procured" (caused) it. See generally: Law Com No 305 (2007), Participating in Crime.

1.6 Some aspects of the present law on the relevance of voluntary intoxication, and indeed certain aspects of our recommendations for reform, raise complex issues. However, we believe that much of the present law, and many of our recommendations for reform, can be stated and understood without too much difficulty, as evidenced by the draft Bill and explanatory note set out in Appendix A.

1.7 Our key purpose in this Part of the Report is to explain the general legal framework and the reasons why reform is necessary. In paragraphs 1.15 to 1.33 we summarise the fundamental components of the current law on intoxication, but we also explain the limitations of our summary with reference to some of the problems with the law. In paragraphs 1.34 to 1.62 we describe the effects of various intoxicants, provide examples of how the law operates in practice, and set out the policy considerations which have shaped the current law.

1.8 A clear understanding of the law and of our recommendations does, however, also require a basic understanding of what is usually required for criminal liability to arise (that is, *without* reference to the question of intoxication). In paragraphs 1.9 to 1.14 we therefore provide an explanation of the framework of criminal liability and the terminology used by criminal lawyers.

CRIMINAL LIABILITY: EXTERNAL AND FAULT ELEMENTS

1.9 To be liable for a criminal offence as a perpetrator, a person (D) must commit the external element of the offence[13] with the required fault (if any).

1.10 Alternatively, if it is alleged that D is liable for an offence perpetrated by another person (P), the prosecution will usually need to prove that D, acting with the fault required for secondary liability, encouraged or assisted P to commit the external element of that offence.[14]

1.11 Broadly speaking, the external element of an offence is the element which does not relate to the question of fault.[15] The external element consists of one or more of the following possible ingredients:

(1) a conduct element (D's act or failure to discharge a legal duty to act);[16]

(2) a consequence element (an effect caused by D's conduct, for example the death of another person);

(3) a circumstances element (for example, a liability requirement that D's conduct has to occur in a public place).

---

[13] Often referred to as the *actus reus*.

[14] The doctrine of secondary liability is explained in fn 12 above.

[15] For some offences, however, it is difficult to distinguish between the fault and the external element. Examples are careless driving and gross negligence manslaughter.

[16] The conduct element is usually considered to contain the further requirement of volition. That is to say, D must voluntarily do the act (or omission) in question to be liable. There can be exceptions to this rule, however: see, eg, *Winzar v Chief Constable of Kent* (1983) *The Times*, 28 March.

1.12 Some offences do not require any fault at all, but where fault is required for criminal liability it may incorporate any or any combination of the following ingredients:

(1) intent as to a consequence,[17] a term which covers D's purpose[18] and also D's foresight of a virtually certain consequence;[19]

(2) knowledge or belief as to a present fact (which exists);[20]

(3) belief as to the highly probable or certain existence of a present or future fact (which may or may not need to exist);[21]

(4) belief as to the possible existence of a present or future fact (which may or may not need to exist),[22] including the concept of "subjective recklessness";[23]

(5) dishonesty;[24]

(6) negligence, requiring proof that D's conduct fell below the standard to be expected of a reasonable (and sober) person;[25]

---

[17] Compare intention as to conduct, which, as explained in fn 16 above, is usually considered to be an aspect of the external element.

[18] The state of mind of a person whose conduct is aimed at achieving something.

[19] The position is that the jury are entitled to infer that D "intended" a consequence from the fact that D foresaw it as a virtually certain result of his or her conduct, even though it was not D's purpose to achieve it: *Woollin* [1999] 1 AC 82.

[20] See, eg, Theft Act 1968, s 22(1) (handling stolen goods) requiring the objective fact that the goods in question are stolen *and* that D knew or believed they were stolen. For the meaning of belief in this context, see *Forsyth* [1997] 2 Cr App R 299, 320 to 321: "the mental acceptance of a fact as true or existing".

[21] Leaving aside the doctrine of joint enterprise, D may be secondarily liable for an offence X committed by P (an objective requirement of such liability) if D provides P with assistance and believes that P *will* commit offence X (see *Johnson v Youden* [1950] 1 KB 544 and, more generally, Law Com No 305 (2007), Participating in Crime, paras B.101 to B.117). With regard to Part 2 of the Serious Crime Act 2007, D may be liable under s 45 for encouraging or assisting the commission of an offence X if, having done an act capable of encouraging or assisting the commission of offence X, D believes another person *will* do the conduct required for offence X (with D's encouragement or assistance) and foresees that that conduct might be done with the fault required for offence X (s 47(3) and (5)(a)(ii)). D may be liable under s 45 even if offence X is never committed.

[22] For example, D is liable for battery if D applies unlawful force to another person (an objective requirement of such liability) believing that his or her conduct *might* result in the application of unlawful force to another person. In addition, as explained in fn 21 above, D will be liable under s 45 of the Serious Crime Act 2007 for encouraging or assisting the commission of an offence X if, having done an act capable of encouraging or assisting the commission of offence X, D believes another person will do the conduct required for offence X (with D's encouragement or assistance) and foresees that that conduct *might* be done with the fault required for offence X (s 47(3) and (5)(a)(ii)). D may be liable under s 45 even if offence X is never committed.

[23] Recklessness is defined with reference to D's awareness of a risk and to D's taking of the risk without justification. An example is provided by the fault requirement of battery (fn 22 above).

[24] See *Ghosh* [1982] QB 1053, where it was held that D is dishonest if (i) reasonable people would regard D's behaviour as dishonest and (ii) D is aware that reasonable people would regard D's behaviour as dishonest. See also Theft Act 1968, s 2.

(7)   objective ("*Caldwell*") recklessness,[26] insofar as the concept still exists.[27]

1.13   Here are some crimes exemplifying these fault and external elements:

(1)   D's liability for the offence of murder requires (i) conduct by D which (ii) caused another person's death, where (iii) D acted with the intention to kill or to cause grievous bodily harm to another person;

(2)   D's liability for the offence of battery requires (i) conduct by D which (ii) constituted or resulted in the application of unlawful force to another person, where (iii) D either intended to apply unlawful force or was subjectively reckless as to the application of such force;

(3)   D's liability for the offence of theft requires (i) the appropriation by D of another person's property, where (ii) D acted dishonestly with (iii) the intention permanently to deprive the other person of the property.

1.14   It is for the prosecution to prove that D committed the external element of the offence charged with the required fault.[28] If this cannot be done, D is entitled to an acquittal in relation to that offence.[29]

---

[25]   Where "gross negligence" is required for liability, D's conduct must fall far below the expected standard: D's conduct must be so bad that it ought to be considered "gross" (a question for the jury); see *Adomako* [1995] 1 AC 171.

[26]   Following *Caldwell* [1982] AC 341. D is *Caldwell* reckless if D is subjectively reckless *or* if D does not foresee the relevant risk but a reasonable person would have foreseen it. (It seems there is no *Caldwell* recklessness, however, if D contemplates the question but wrongly concludes that there is no risk.)

[27]   It remains to be seen whether there is now any place for objective recklessness in English criminal law in the light of the House of Lords' judgment in *G* [2003] UKHL 50, [2004] 1 AC 1034, where the concept was finally abandoned in relation to allegations of criminal damage. The objective *Caldwell* test had previously been held to apply to the use of the word "reckless" in all statutory offences (*Lawrence* [1982] AC 510, 525 by Lord Diplock); and the decision in *G* was expressly limited to the Criminal Damage Act 1971 ([28] by Lord Bingham, who expressly approved *Lawrence*, and [43] by Lord Steyn). Nevertheless, it is quite possible that the subjective approach now adopted for criminal damage will be followed in relation to other statutory offences defined with reference to "recklessness". It is to be noted that in *A-G's Reference (No 3 of 2003)* [2004] EWCA Crim 868, [2005] QB 73, a case relating to the common law offence of misconduct in public office, the Court of Appeal concluded that *G* contained "general principles" that were binding on it ([12] and [45]).

[28]   However, if D relies on the common law defence of insanity to show that he or she did not act with the required fault, it is for D to prove the defence.

[29]   D may, however, be liable for an alternative offence. Where D is charged with murder, D may be liable for manslaughter rather than murder, notwithstanding his or her proven or admitted fault for murder, on the ground that he or she has a partial defence such as provocation.

INTOXICATION AND CRIMINAL LIABILITY: THE BASIC COMPONENTS

1.15   It is important to make one thing clear at the outset. There is no common law or statutory "defence of intoxication". That is to say, the simple fact that D was voluntarily intoxicated at the time he or she allegedly committed the offence charged does not provide D with a "defence". Equally, the fact that D acted involuntarily in a state of automatism caused by voluntary intoxication does not allow D to rely on the defence of automatism.[30]

1.16   However, if D's state of intoxication was such that D did not act with the subjective fault (culpable state of mind) required for liability by the definition of the offence it *may* be possible for D to secure an acquittal for that reason.

1.17   The word "may" in the preceding paragraph is crucially important in this context. If D did not act with the subjective fault required for liability by the definition of the offence because of voluntary intoxication, it does not necessarily follow that D will be able to avoid liability. Voluntary intoxication prevents proof of criminal liability only if the subjective fault required by the definition of the offence is of a particular type; that is, it is one of the culpable states of mind labelled by the courts (confusingly) as a "specific intent". An example of a state of mind labelled as a "specific intent" is the fault element of murder, the intent to kill or cause grievous bodily harm.[31] The prosecution must always prove that D acted with one of these two states of mind, and if the prosecution cannot discharge this burden of proof, because of the evidence of D's intoxicated state, then D cannot be convicted of murder. Offences which do not require the prosecution to prove that D acted with a "specific intent" have come to be known (again, confusingly) as offences of "basic intent".

1.18   If the subjective fault required by the definition of the offence charged has not been labelled as a "specific intent", then the fact that D was voluntarily intoxicated at the time D allegedly committed the offence is irrelevant to his or her liability for it. This means that the jury (or other tribunal of fact) is required to consider the hypothetical question whether, at the relevant time, D *would* have been acting with the fault required by the definition of the offence if D had not been intoxicated. The mere fact of being voluntarily intoxicated cannot simply be treated as a substitute for the requirement that subjective fault be proved.

---

[30] Automatism is the general defence to liability based on the fact that D did not act with the volition usually required for criminal liability, but it cannot be relied on if D's condition was culpably self-induced (eg, by the voluntary consumption of alcohol).

[31] See para 1.13(1) above.

1.19   For example, battery is defined with a fault element of intention or subjective recklessness as to the application of unlawful force (that is, a requirement that D intended or foresaw the possible application of unlawful force).[32] Recklessness so defined is not regarded as a "specific intent", so if D is charged with battery the tribunal of fact must consider whether D would have foreseen the possibility of unlawful force being applied if he or she had been sober. If D would have foreseen that possibility if sober, D is liable. It is irrelevant to D's liability that D did not actually foresee that possibility if the lack of foresight was caused by D's state of voluntary intoxication (even though, as noted above, proof of subjective recklessness is required by the definition of the offence).

1.20   It follows from the foregoing analysis that D is never able to rely on his or her state of voluntary intoxication if D's argument as to its relevance is simply that it caused D's inhibitions to be reduced or D's moral vision to be blurred. The courts do not consider these effects of voluntary intoxication to be relevant to the determination of D's liability.[33] In other words, if it is proved that D committed the external element of an offence with the fault required for liability, D is guilty of the offence even though D would not have committed it if his or her inhibitions had not been reduced or his or her moral vision had not been blurred by the voluntary consumption of an intoxicant.

1.21   Our introduction to the core components of the law on intoxication and criminal liability explains the relevance, or irrelevance, of voluntary intoxication to the definitional elements of the offence charged. It does not, however, explain whether voluntary intoxication can be relevant to a general defence (such as duress) or an analogous concept which can properly be regarded as a general defence (such as self-defence).[34] It will be seen in Part 2[35] that a mistaken belief on which D seeks to rely in support of any such defence is irrelevant if it was caused by voluntary intoxication, regardless of the offence charged and therefore regardless of whether the fault element is or is not a "specific intent". Again, this must mean that the jury (or other tribunal of fact) should consider the hypothetical question whether, at the relevant time, D would have made the same mistake if D had been sober. However, a complication here is that a different rule applies in relation to at least one non-general defence to liability.[36]

---

[32]   See para 1.13(2) above.

[33]   Nor, it will be seen, are these effects of intoxication considered to be relevant if D's state of intoxication was *involuntary*, if D acted with the fault required by the definition of the offence charged. This aspect of the law is addressed in Part 4.

[34]   This distinction is not significant for the purposes of this introduction, but an explanation is provided in fn 70 in Part 3 below.

[35]   Paragraphs 2.47 to 2.60 below.

[36]   Criminal Damage Act 1971, s 5(2)–(3); see paras 2.94 to 2.97 below.

1.22 We have already pointed out that a distinction needs to be drawn between the usual case of voluntary intoxication and the rare case of involuntary intoxication, and the law does indeed recognise such a distinction.[37] If D did not act with the subjective fault required by the definition of the offence because of involuntary intoxication, then D cannot be convicted of the offence. This is a rule with no exceptions: no distinction is drawn between culpable states of mind labelled as "specific intents" and other culpable states of mind the prosecution has to prove.

1.23 Similarly, if D was in a state of automatism caused by involuntary intoxication, D may rely on the defence of automatism. The rule which prevents D from relying on the defence if it was caused by voluntary intoxication[38] does not apply if D's state of automatism was caused by involuntary intoxication. Similarly, if D wishes to rely on a mistaken understanding of the facts to support a general defence D is relying on to avoid liability, D may do so if his or her mistaken belief was caused by involuntary intoxication.

1.24 Our attempt in the preceding paragraphs to summarise the core components of the law on intoxication might suggest that the legal framework can be readily ascertained from the appellate courts' judgments and that the law is conceptually clear and sound. Unfortunately this is not so.

1.25 Our summary explains that different rules apply depending on whether D's state of intoxication was voluntary or involuntary and that the distinction is therefore of crucial importance. However, there is a great deal of ambiguity over the demarcation between the concepts of voluntary and involuntary intoxication, undermining the usefulness of our summary as an introductory guide to the law. This is a problem which needs to be addressed.[39]

1.26 It is also difficult to find in the case law a generally accepted test for juries and magistrates' courts as to the relevance of D's self-induced state of intoxication when assessing his or her criminal liability. We have set out what the test *must* be, for which support can certainly be found in some judgments of the appellate courts; but the case law and some academic writers suggest an alternative test which, if correct, would be unworkable. We believe that the criminal courts and the general public should be provided with a clearer, more accessible and comprehensive test for determining the relevance of intoxication to criminal liability.

1.27 Another problem with our summary is that it does not even begin to explain the test for determining whether a subjective fault element is or is not to be labelled as a "specific intent". In the absence of such clarification, our summary is far less useful than might be supposed. The case law provides some guidance, but there is no single, uniform test to be applied, and this degree of uncertainty in the law is unacceptable.

---

[37] Paragraphs 2.75 to 2.89 below.

[38] Paragraph 1.15 (and fn 30) above.

[39] It will be seen in paras 2.85 to 2.86 below that an unsatisfactory distinction has been drawn at common law between dangerous and soporific drugs for determining the nature of D's intoxication (with no criteria for determining how any particular drug should be categorised). For example, the benzo-diazepines, such as Valium, are taken clinically to increase sedation, but they can also cause aggression. See generally Law Com No 229 (1995), Legislating the Criminal Code: Intoxication and Criminal Liability, para 5.42.

1.28 A related point is that our summary merely alludes to the present confusion caused by the terminology which has developed in this context, that is, the references to "offences of basic intent" (voluntary intoxication irrelevant) and "offences of specific intent" (intoxication relevant). We believe that this distinction is ambiguous, misleading and confusing, and that it should be abandoned.

1.29 Additionally, our summary does not explain the test to be applied if D is charged on the basis that he or she was an accessory rather than a perpetrator. This is because the test for accessories has never been articulated in the case law, notwithstanding the practical importance of the doctrine of secondary liability. It is possible to surmise what the test must sensibly be, but it will be seen later in this Report that recent reforms introduced by Parliament[40] undermine the argument for a sensible interpretation, suggesting that D could be liable for a murder committed by some other person even though D did *not* act with the fault required for murder and, on account of voluntary intoxication, did not even foresee the possibility that murder would be committed by the perpetrator.[41] If this is the law, it is unacceptable. If it is not, the legal position must at least be clarified.

1.30 However, our summary does explain that the appellate courts have not been consistent in their approach to the defences to criminal liability. If this difference is not to generate anomalies, it needs to be addressed.

1.31 In short, we believe the present law on intoxication and criminal liability is far from satisfactory. The following five issues require particular attention as they are central to the recommendations we make later in this Report:

(1) the question whether D's intoxication should be classified as "voluntary" or "involuntary";

(2) the question whether the fault element in the definition of the offence charged is or is not one to which voluntary intoxication should be considered relevant;

(3) the question whether voluntary intoxication should be considered relevant to the defences to which D's state of mind may be relevant;

(4) the test to be applied in cases where voluntary intoxication is not relevant to the determination of D's criminal liability; and

(5) the test to be applied in cases where it is alleged that D did not perpetrate the offence charged but encouraged or assisted a perpetrator to commit it.[42]

---

[40] Part 2 of the Serious Crime Act 2007.

[41] See paras 2.98 to 2.105 below.

[42] It will be seen that a similar problem arises under Part 2 of the Serious Crime Act 2007, for cases where D is charged with an inchoate offence of encouraging or assisting crime.

1.32 In our view the present law does not satisfactorily address these central issues and is in need of reform. We explain the problems with the law in more detail in Part 2 of this Report and set out our recommendations for reform in Part 3. The draft Bill appended to this Report[43] provides the means by which our recommendations could be taken forward and given effect.

1.33 There is a further aspect of the law which needs to be addressed, but in our view does not need to be reformed. This is the question whether D's *involuntary* state of intoxication at the time he or she allegedly committed the offence charged should *excuse* D from liability, on the ground that, whilst D acted with the relevant fault for liability, he or she committed the offence because the intoxicant adversely affected his or her inhibitions or moral awareness.[44] We consider this specific issue in Part 4.

CRIMINAL LIABILITY AND INTOXICATION

1.34 Under this heading we summarise the various ways in which alcohol and other drugs can affect human behaviour.[45] We also explain in a little more detail the relationship between voluntary intoxication and criminal liability and introduce the relevant principles and policy considerations which have shaped the law. In our examples we focus on offences against the person because of the strong link, explained earlier, between voluntary intoxication and violent crime.

Species of intoxication

1.35 Alcohol is a cortical depressant which inhibits the cerebral functions associated with orderly community behaviour and fine critical judgments.[46] Drugs such as heroin and morphine, which depress the central nervous system, may also give rise to drowsiness and an inability to concentrate, and may allay anxieties.[47] In excess, however, depressants may result in psychosis and aggressive behaviour.

1.36 Stimulants, such as cocaine and amphetamine, may, if taken in excess, lead to impairment of judgment and reasoning, give rise to feelings of persecution and possibly result in delusions and hallucinations. Distortions of perception and hallucinations are also a likely consequence of taking hallucinogens such as LSD and "magic mushrooms".

---

[43] Appendix A (with explanatory notes).

[44] The question of D's liability in a case where he or she acted with the fault required for liability, but committed the offence because of reduced inhibitions arising from *voluntary* intoxication, requires no analysis. D should clearly be liable for an offence in any such case.

[45] Our summary draws on Mackay, *Mental Condition Defences in the Criminal Law* (1995) p 145.

[46] Other possible effects of alcohol are "pathological intoxication", where D behaves in an uncharacteristic manner, and "alcoholic amnesia" amounting to a total or partial inability to remember what happened while drunk. See Mackay, *Mental Condition Defences in the Criminal Law* (1995) p 147.

[47] The fact that D's anxieties are allayed as a result of having taken an opiate, giving D enhanced self-confidence, may be of particular significance for some types of offending, particularly if D suffers no significant deterioration in his or her mental ability or manual dexterity (see MG Paulsen, "Intoxication as a Defense to Crime" (1961) *University of Illinois Law Forum* 1, 23 to 24).

1.37   Alcohol or other drugs may therefore intoxicate a person (D) with normal mental faculties in three different ways.[48]

1.38   First, D may experience nothing more than a feeling of enhanced self-confidence and reduced inhibitions, where D is aware of what he or she is doing and the possible consequences of his or her conduct, but is less inclined to act in accordance with the constraints which would ordinarily keep D within the bounds of civilised behaviour when sober. This may mean that D satisfies the external and fault elements of an offence, and D's only claim to exculpation is that D would not have committed the offence if he or she had been sober:

Example 1A

D is charged with having committed a battery against V.[49] The defence may claim that, although it can be proved that D did an act which resulted in the application of unlawful force to another person (V), and that D intended to apply unlawful force to V, D acted in this way only because he or she had been drinking strong lager and that, if sober, D would have avoided any confrontation with V.

As explained above, D cannot rely on his or her state of self-intoxication in this example to avoid liability. D is guilty of battery.

1.39   Secondly, an intoxicant may cause D to misapprehend risks and/or mistakenly perceive the surrounding circumstances or the consequences of his or her conduct. This may mean that, whilst it can be proved that D committed the external element of an offence, it is not possible to prove that D had the culpable state of mind for liability according to its definitional requirements:

Example 1B

D stabs V with a knife causing V's death. D was aiming to strike V's hand with the weapon, but, due to intoxication, stabbed V in the heart.

Example 1C

D stabs V with a knife causing V's death. Due to intoxication, D wrongly believed that V was a mannequin.

---

[48]   The effect of alcohol or other drugs on a person who is affected by a mental disorder may increase the risk that he or she will act violently, although much depends on the nature of the disorder . See, for example, the paper by the National Programme on Forensic Mental Health Research and Development, "Dual Diagnosis of Mental Disorder and Substance Misuse" (2007) pp 14 to 16.

[49]   Paragraph 1.13(2) above.

D is not liable for the offence of murder[50] in these examples if D did not intend to kill or cause grievous bodily harm to V or any other person.

1.40   In other words, in accordance with conventional legal principle, if D intended to cause nothing more than minor bodily harm to V, or serious damage to something other than a person, D is not guilty of murder because D did not act with the fault required by the definition of this offence.[51] The intentions required for murder are regarded as "specific intents" which must *always* be proved.[52] However, D could be liable for one or more less serious offences.[53]

1.41   In the situation where D fatally stabs V with a knife but does not act with the fault required for murder:

(1)   D is liable for battery[54] if, notwithstanding his or her self-induced state of intoxication, D intended to apply unlawful force to V. If D's battery caused V's death, D is also liable for manslaughter.

(2)   D is liable for battery even though, because of D's self-induced state of intoxication, D did not intend to apply unlawful force to V or foresee the risk that V (or anyone else) would suffer the application of unlawful force, so long as D *would* have foreseen that risk if D had been sober. If D's battery caused V's death, D is liable for manslaughter.

1.42   It is important to note that D is guilty of manslaughter in the second situation described, which encompasses example 1C, even though D did *not* act with the subjective fault usually required for the offence of battery (and therefore for manslaughter predicated on battery).

1.43   As mentioned earlier, the law recognises that the concept of subjective recklessness is such that, while it ordinarily requires that D foresaw the relevant risk, it may be established on an alternative basis. Recklessness is not regarded as a "specific intent". So, D is considered to have been reckless for the purposes of the offence of battery (and therefore manslaughter) if, though the relevant risk was not foreseen by D on account of voluntary intoxication, D would have foreseen that risk if D had not been voluntarily intoxicated.

1.44   However, if D did not act with the intention or recklessness required by the definition of the offence charged because of his or her *involuntary* state of intoxication, D will not in law be liable for the offence. The alternative basis of establishing liability referred to in paragraph 1.43 does not apply if D's state of intoxication was not self-induced. For example, D is not liable for battery if D neither intended to apply unlawful force to V nor foresaw the possibility of unlawful force being applied to V, if that lack of intention or awareness was caused by D's consumption of a soft drink which had been surreptitiously laced with a drug.

---

[50]   Paragraph 1.13(1) above.

[51]   Similarly, D is not liable for murder if D took V to be an ape and intended to kill or seriously injure that (imagined) ape.

[52]   Paragraph 1.17 above.

[53]   See paras 2.35 to 2.42 below.

[54]   Paragraph 1.13(2) above.

1.45 So far we have explained two ways in which a drug may have an effect on D. A third way is where D is rendered so intoxicated that he or she is in a state of automatism. In other words, it may not be possible for the prosecution to prove that D acted voluntarily.[55]

1.46 The general defence of automatism allows D to avoid liability on the basis that he or she did not act voluntarily. D cannot rely on this defence, however, if the state of automatism was caused by voluntary intoxication.[56]

Example 1D

D voluntarily consumes 20 pints of strong lager and, as a result, enters into a state of automatism. D wanders into a crowd of people, striking out at them and hitting one individual.

1.47 In this example, D is guilty of battery because his state of automatism was culpably self-induced. If D had not drunk 20 pints of strong lager, D would have been acting voluntarily and would have foreseen the risk of applying unlawful force to another person.

1.48 It should by now be apparent that the criminal courts' approach to the relevance of intoxication to criminal liability is in some respects based on simple logic in the application of the definitions of crime, but in other respects is based on broader considerations of public policy (albeit considerations linked to legal principles).

1.49 An approach based entirely on simple definitional logic would in all cases focus solely on the legal requirements of criminal offences. It would allow D to rely on his intoxication in any case where the offence charged requires proof of a particular state of mind or volition[57] (which includes nearly all serious offences against the person).

1.50 Adopting this approach to criminal liability would mean taking the following line of argument in analysing the situation where D fatally stabs V without the fault required for murder. D would not be guilty of battery if D neither intended to apply unlawful force nor foresaw the possibility of applying unlawful force, if D's awareness of that possibility was blocked by his or her self-induced state of intoxication (even if D would have foreseen the possibility had he or she been sober).

---

[55] As explained in fn 16 above, volition is an implicit requirement of the conduct element of most offences.

[56] See fn 30 above. Of course, if D's state of automatism meant that D did not act with the culpable state of mind required for liability, and that state of mind is regarded as a "specific intent", then D is not liable for the offence charged for that reason.

[57] Insofar as the intoxication affected D's state of mind in a relevant respect or D's capacity for voluntary conduct.

1.51   The approach based on definitional logic is associated with a so-called "subjective" approach to criminal liability. On this approach, it is D's actual state of mind at the time of the alleged offence which is relevant to guilt. What D's state of mind would have been, had D been sober, is not relevant.

1.52   The same strictly logical approach would also mean that if D was in a state of automatism through the voluntary consumption of alcohol or other drugs, D would not be liable for any criminal offence requiring volition. It would not be possible to prove that D acted voluntarily if D was in a state of automatism, and, as already explained, volition is a definitional requirement of most criminal offences.

1.53   The problem with a strictly logical, subjective approach to criminal liability, if accepted, is that it would have the effect of providing D with a complete answer to *any* serious offence requiring proof of a culpable state of mind. In other words, an aggressive drunk or drug abuser could cause any kind or degree of damage or injury without incurring serious criminal liability, merely because his or her level of self-induced intoxication was such that he or she might not have acted with the foresight of risk (or the volition) ordinarily required for liability.[58]

1.54   Whatever strict legal logic might dictate, we suspect that most people would agree, as we do, with Professor Glanville Williams' observation that, "it would be inimical to the safety of all of us if the judges announced that anyone could gain exemption from the criminal law by getting drunk".[59] In this area of the law, concerns about public safety need to be taken into consideration, even if they offend against subjectivists' logical arguments.

1.55   We are therefore unable to support the idea that the strictly logical approach should always govern the imposition of criminal liability in cases where it is alleged that D, in a self-induced state of intoxication, committed a violent offence. Given the culpability associated with knowingly and voluntarily becoming intoxicated, and the associated increase in the known risk of aggressive behaviour, there is a compelling argument for imposing criminal liability to the extent reflected by that culpability. The imposition of such criminal liability is morally justifiable in principle, and warranted by the desirability of ensuring public safety and deterring harmful conduct.

1.56   However, we accept that it would be unprincipled, and indeed unworkable, never to allow D to rely on voluntary intoxication to avoid liability. D's intoxicated understanding of the world cannot and should not always be discarded in favour of the view D would have had if sober. An "absolutist" approach of this kind, which would focus solely on D's conduct and its effects, but would disregard D's state of mind where affected by voluntary intoxication, might contribute in some small way to the reduction of the social evil of drink or drug-fuelled violent crime and reassure the public. However, it could result in D being convicted of offences such as murder when D's culpability came nowhere close to the requirements for legal liability. To permit such a degree of mismatch between the level of culpability and the level of the offence committed would be wrong.

---

[58]   There could, however, be relatively minor liability for an offence not requiring proof of subjective fault (if D was not acting as an automaton).

[59]   G. Williams, *Textbook of Criminal Law* (2nd ed, 1983) p 466. It is not strictly correct to refer to an "exemption" from liability, but Williams' argument is nonetheless a powerful one.

1.57   Adopting a policy of absolutism would involve disregarding the fact that D, in a drunken state, genuinely believed that he was stabbing a mannequin when stabbing a friend, and would hold D liable for murder on the basis that, if D had been sober, D would have realised that he or she was stabbing a real person, attributing to D a non-existent intention to kill or seriously harm another person. Certainly, in such an example, it cannot be denied that D should bear moral responsibility for being in a self-induced state of intoxication, and for the real harm he or she has caused, but D's culpability cannot be equated with the culpability of a person who commits homicide with the intention to kill or seriously harm another human being. The absolutist approach, if accepted, would equate the moral culpability associated with self-induced intoxication to the moral culpability required for *any* crime, even murder. Such a disproportion between culpability and the extent of liability cannot be introduced into the criminal law.

1.58   Given the unattractiveness of both the strictly logical approach to criminal liability and the absolutist alternative, it should come as no surprise that English law has rejected both these extreme approaches in favour of an intermediate position. To put it another way, English law has adopted the purely logical view for some offences, focusing solely on the definitional requirements of the offence charged, but has employed the absolutist approach in relation to other offences.

1.59   The absolutist approach has been adopted only if there is no or no significant mismatch between the culpability ordinarily required for liability (in accordance with the definitional requirements of the offence) and the culpability associated with committing the external element of the offence in a self-induced state of intoxication. Moreover, although the strictly logical approach may allow D to avoid liability for one offence, if the prosecution cannot prove the required state of mind, there will usually be an alternative offence for which D can be held liable (on the same facts) through an application of the absolutist approach.

1.60   Thus, some subjective fault elements, such as purpose as to a consequence and knowledge of a fact – states of mind which, as explained above, have come to be known as "specific intents" – must always be proved for D to be liable for the offence and can never be simply attributed to D. However, subjective recklessness need not be proved if D would have been aware of the relevant risk of harm if D had not been voluntarily intoxicated. As explained already, offences which do not require proof of a "specific intent" have come to be known as offences of "basic intent".

1.61   The rationale for this approach is that the advertent recklessness in voluntarily choosing to become intoxicated, and becoming a greater danger to society, may be equated, morally, with the subjective (advertent) recklessness usually required for liability. This is the legal principle underpinning the absolutist approach.

1.62   That said, the courts' rejection of the strictly logical approach has engendered controversy on account of what is perceived to be the judiciary's willingness to allow considerations of public policy to override the requirements of definitional logic without reference to legal principle at all. Unsurprisingly, therefore, this is an area of the law which has already been considered by a number of English law reform bodies, including the Law Commission.[60]

THE COMMISSION'S PREVIOUS RECOMMENDATIONS

1.63   The Law Commission undertook a thorough review of the law on intoxication prior to publishing its 1992 consultation paper Intoxication and Criminal Liability.[61] Following consultation, the Commission's final recommendations were set out in its 1995 report Legislating the Criminal Code: Intoxication and Criminal Liability ("the 1995 report").[62]

1.64   The recommendations in the 1995 report were designed to supersede the intoxication provisions in the Draft Criminal Law (Intoxication) Bill appended to the Commission's report Legislating the Criminal Code: Offences Against the Person and General Principles (1993), Law Com No 218,[63] and the relevant clause in the Commission's original Draft Criminal Code Bill.[64]

1.65   The Commission's ultimate conclusion in the 1995 report was that "the present law should be codified, with some minor modifications, and that in areas of doubt it should be clarified". [65] The underlying rationale was to make the law "simpler, fairer and cheaper to use".[66]

1.66   However, the Commission's Draft Criminal Law (Intoxication) Bill appended to the 1995 report has never been presented to Parliament; and the provisions were not included in the Government's draft proposals for reforming the law governing violent conduct. In its 1998 consultation paper, Violence, Reforming the Offences Against the Person Act 1861, the Home Office commented that the Government had considered the Commission's recommendations and Draft Criminal Law (Intoxication) Bill but had concluded "that they were unnecessarily complex for the purposes of [its Offences Against the Person] Bill".[67]

---

[60]   The question was addressed in the Butler Committee's Report of the Committee on Mentally Abnormal Offenders (1975) Cmnd 6244 and in the Criminal Law Revision Committee's Fourteenth Report, Offences Against the Person (1980) Cmnd 7844. See generally Appendix B. For the Law Commission's involvement, see below.

[61]   Law Commission Consultation Paper No 127.

[62]   Law Com No 229.

[63]   See Law Com No 229, para 1.13.

[64]   A Criminal Code for England and Wales: Report and Draft Criminal Code Bill (1989) Law Com No 177, Vol 1, cl 22.

[65]   Law Com No 229, para 1.3.

[66]   Above.

[67]   Paragraph 3.23.

1.67 More than a decade after the publication of the 1995 report we are still of the view, broadly speaking, that codification with clarification and modifications is the right approach. However, we do not now believe that *all* aspects the present law governing intoxication and criminal liability should be incorporated into legislation. We accept that the Commission's previous attempt to give effect to its policy might legitimately be regarded as unduly complex; and one of the reasons for this is that the Commission previously saw merit in the creation of a comprehensive code.

1.68 We have therefore decided to revisit this important area of the criminal law with a view to providing Parliament with an entirely new draft Bill which, while broadly consistent with the policy underpinning the 1995 Bill, seeks to address the criticisms levelled against it.

THE STRUCTURE OF THIS REPORT AND OUR RECOMMENDATIONS

1.69 In Part 2 we provide a more detailed account of the current state of the law on the relevance of voluntary intoxication to fault and criminal liability. We also address the situation where D acts without the fault required for the offence charged because of involuntary intoxication. An example would be where D is forced to consume alcohol against his or her will, and, as a result of his or her intoxicated state, commits the external element of battery without the intention or subjective recklessness ordinarily required by the definition of the offence.

1.70 In Part 3 we summarise the Commission's earlier recommendations for reform and set out our present recommendations on the relevance of voluntary and involuntary intoxication to criminal liability. We consider the position both for alleged perpetrators and for alleged accessories (under the doctrine of secondary liability).

1.71 In Part 4 we focus on an area which was omitted from the 1995 report, as explained above.[68] This issue is whether D should be afforded the benefit of a defence if he or she committed the external element of an offence with the required fault because D's inhibitions had been removed, or moral awareness clouded, by involuntary intoxication. For example, should D, whose orange juice was laced with alcohol, and whose inhibitions were reduced as a result, be able to avoid liability for the sexual offence subsequently committed by him whilst drunk on the ground that he would not have committed the offence if his inhibitions had not been reduced or removed? Our recommendation is that there should be no such defence.[69]

1.72 Our recommendations are summarised in Part 5.

1.73 In Appendix A we set out our new draft Criminal Law (Intoxication) Bill with explanatory notes on its various provisions.

---

[68] See para 1.33 above.

[69] As explained in fn 44 above, no similar issue arises in the context of *voluntary* intoxication.

1.74 Any legislation which seeks to codify most, if not all, of the present law must address all criminal offences requiring proof of subjective fault, and must cater for the various ways in which an offender may participate in the commission of a criminal offence (and the different rules which apply to the different modes of participation). Such legislation must also provide rules for defences, regardless of whether the offence charged has a requirement of subjective fault, and distinguish between defences and a denial of fault. Our new draft Bill does all of these things in what we consider to be a concise and readily understandable fashion. In addition, we believe that:

(1) our new draft Bill is more comprehensible and yet also closer to being a comprehensive code, in broad terms, than the draft Bill the Commission published in 1995;[70] and

(2) its provisions would, if given the force of law, be a vast improvement over the present common law on intoxication and criminal liability.

1.75 In Appendix B we summarise other recommendations for reform in England and Wales.

1.76 In Appendix C we summarise the approach adopted in some other common law jurisdictions.

---

[70] That is to say, although our new draft Bill does not seek to address all the unusual factual scenarios covered by the 1995 Bill, it does encompass both primary liability (perpetrators) and secondary liability (accessories).

PART 2
INTOXICATION AND FAULT – THE PRESENT LAW AND ITS LIMITATIONS

INTRODUCTION

2.1 In this Part we set out in more detail the present common law rules governing the extent to which a person can be criminally liable for an offence requiring fault if he or she lacked that fault on account of:

(1) voluntary (self-induced) intoxication, or

(2) involuntary intoxication.

TERMINOLOGY: OFFENCES OF SPECIFIC AND BASIC INTENT

2.2 As we explained in Part 1,[1] the criminal courts have drawn a distinction between offences of "basic intent" (or "general intent") and offences of "specific intent". Offences of "specific intent" always require proof that D acted with a particular state of mind, that is, the state of mind required by the legal definition of the fault element.[2] By contrast, it is possible for D to be convicted of a "basic intent" offence even if D did not act with the state of mind required by the legal definition of the fault element. As explained in paragraphs 1.17 to 1.19 above, this is possible if D was voluntarily intoxicated at the relevant time and D would have had the required state of mind if he or she had been sober.

2.3 The terms "specific intent" and "basic intent" are not particularly enlightening, however, because they have been interpreted by different judges and academic writers to mean different things.[3] As noted by the Commission in the 1995 report:[4] "[t]here are a number of alternative theories as to the meanings of these two terms, and the criteria for categorising offences in this way; and there is a great deal of uncertainty as a result."[5] The Commission might have added that the distinction is also profoundly misleading. Nevertheless, the distinction continues to be drawn, and is of great practical significance when considering the relevance of self-induced intoxication to criminal liability.

---

[1] See paras 1.17, 1.28 and 1.60.

[2] Still often referred to as the "*mens rea*" of the offence.

[3] See, in particular, the leading case of *DPP v Majewski* [1977] AC 443, 478. Williams, *Textbook of Criminal Law* (2nd ed, 1983) p 471, notes that in *DPP v Majewski* "the law lords . . . while unanimous that there is such a distinction . . . failed to agree on a definition of the two intents".

[4] Legislating the Criminal Code: Intoxication and Criminal Liability (1995), Law Com No 229; see para 1.63 above.

[5] Law Com No 229, above, para 3.17.

2.4 One possible way of explaining the classification of "intents", which has superficial appeal, and for which support can be found in the case law, is to say that an offence is one of "basic intent" if it has an express or implicit requirement of volition (the "intent" in question being the intention to act or not act as the case may be) but it does not otherwise have a specific *fault* requirement of intention.[6] Adopting this interpretation, an offence is an offence of "specific intent" if it does have a specific fault requirement of intention (in addition to the usual "basic intent").

2.5 There is a problem with this analysis, however, which is one of the sources of the misleading character of the distinction between "specific" and "basic" intents. This is that the courts have developed the classification of offences so that neither offences of "basic intent" nor offences of "specific intent" necessarily require proof of an intention of any kind.

2.6 For example, a teacher (D) supervising some pupils near a cliff edge might be unable to prevent him or herself from falling asleep through boredom or tiredness. This would in all probability be regarded as gross negligence, and for that reason could result in a manslaughter conviction[7] if a child died because of the absence of effective supervision. But falling asleep is hardly a voluntary act if one is trying to stay awake, and yet gross negligence manslaughter is classified as an offence of "basic intent". Accordingly, if D's tiredness was caused by the voluntary consumption of alcohol, that state of intoxication would provide D with no defence to a charge of manslaughter. On the contrary, it would tend to show that D's conduct was sufficiently neglectful to justify a conviction for the offence. The important point is that it is irrelevant to the categorisation of gross negligence manslaughter as a crime of "basic intent" that there was no "intentional" conduct on D's part in contributing to the death of the child by falling asleep on duty.

2.7 We will see that the notion of "basic intent" is really a negative rather than a positive designation of an offence. It signifies that, whatever the fault element required to be proved respecting some aspect or all of the external element of the offence in question, it does not include one of a range of states of mind regarded in law as "specific intents".

---

[6] In *DPP v Newbury* [1977] AC 500, 509, Lord Salmon said: "what is called a basic intention . . . is an intention to do the acts which constitute the crime." In *Heard* [2007] EWCA Crim 125, [2008] QB 43, the trial judge equated the requirement of basic intent with the notion of acting "deliberately rather than accidentally", a ruling upheld on appeal (paras 8, 23 and 32).

[7] Gross negligence manslaughter. See Part 1, fn 25.

2.8   Equally, the categorisation of an offence as one of "specific intent" does not necessarily require proof of a specific fault element of intention. It may do, as in the crime of murder, which requires proof of an intention to kill or cause grievous bodily harm;[8] but the notion of specific "intent" includes other states of mind such as a requirement of knowledge or belief that something is the case. It may also encompass the common law test of "foresight of a possibility" required for D's secondary liability as an accessory[9] in a case where the offence perpetrated by P, during the course of a joint venture, is one of "specific intent".[10] In *Heard*[11] the Court of Appeal recently went so far as to suggest (we believe, wrongly) that the notion of "specific intent" also extends to a requirement of recklessness as to something beyond the requirements of the offence's external element and which, for that reason, could be classified as an "ulterior intent".[12]

2.9   Conversely, an explicit requirement of intention in the definition of an offence does not necessarily mean that the offence is one of "specific intent". In *Heard*[13] the Court of Appeal held that "intentionally" in section 3 of the Sexual Offences Act 2003 (sexual assault) requires nothing more than proof that D's conduct was non-accidental and was not to be interpreted as a requirement of "specific intent".[14] It follows that rape is also still an offence of "basic intent" even though, to be liable, D must have "intentionally" penetrated the vagina, anus or mouth of another person.[15]

---

[8]   Paragraph 1.13(1) above.

[9]   The doctrine of secondary liability is summarised in fn 12 of Part 1 above.

[10]   If, for example, D provides P with encouragement or assistance in relation to a joint venture to burgle V's house, and during the burglary P murders V, D is liable for murder (an offence of "specific intent") if D foresaw the *possibility* that murder would be committed during the course of the venture: *Chan Wing-Siu* [1985] 1 AC 168, *Powell and Daniels* [1999] 1 AC 1. See paras 2.98 to 2.101 below.

[11]   [2007] EWCA Crim 125, [2008] QB 43, para 31.

[12]   The Court of Appeal took the view that an "ulterior intent" so defined is a "specific intent" (whether or not the state of mind in question requires proof of intent), although it was also accepted that the term "specific intent" encompasses other states of mind too. We take the view that this suggestion, that recklessness can be a "specific intent", is contrary to an established interpretation of the distinction between "basic" and "specific" intents and should be disregarded (see para 2.20 below). On this point, the decision in *Caldwell* [1982] AC 341 is still good law.

[13]   [2007] EWCA Crim 125, [2008] QB 43.

[14]   See also *MacPherson* [1973] RTR 157, fn 22 below.

[15]   Section 1(1) of the Sexual Offences Act 2003. The previous definition of rape in section 1 of the Sexual Offences Act 1956, which did not include any explicit reference to "intention", was considered to be an offence of "basic intent". The decision in *Heard* [2007] EWCA Crim 125, [2008] QB 43 suggests that the inclusion of "intentionally" in s 1(1) of the Sexual Offences Act 2003 is nothing more than an explicit reference to the (previously implicit) external element requirement of volition rather than an aspect of the offence's fault element. However, in the recent case of *G* [2008] UKHL 37, [2008] 1 WLR 1379, at paras 3, 21 and 46, the equivalent requirement of intentional penetration in s 5(1)(a) of the 2003 Act (rape of a child under 13) was assumed to be a *fault* requirement (by Lord Hoffmann, Lord Hope and Baroness Hale respectively).

2.10   Moreover, an offence which can be committed with a "specific intent" is not to be regarded as an offence of "specific intent" if a conviction for it can also be founded on proof of recklessness.[16] Thus, common assault is an offence of "basic intent" even though it may also be committed with a "specific intent".[17] D is liable for assault if he or she intends to cause V to apprehend immediate, unlawful force *or* if he or she foresees a risk that V will apprehend such force.[18]

2.11   It is important to reiterate that the notion of "specific intent" extends to some states of mind which are not intentions. It has been held to encompass the "knowledge or belief" requirement for the offence of handling stolen goods[19] and almost certainly extends to the concept of "dishonesty".[20] That said, the courts have on occasion demonstrated a disinclination to categorise crimes as "specific intent" offences if they do not have to, thereby limiting the extent to which voluntary intoxication can be relied on as evidence of lack of fault.

2.12   So, where a knowledge or belief requirement is only an implicit rather than an explicit part of the fault element in an offence, the courts have been willing to categorise the offence as one of "basic intent". This was the approach adopted in *DPP v Kellet*.[21] In that case D was charged with allowing an unmuzzled dangerous dog to be in a public place, contrary to section 1 of the Dangerous Dogs Act 1991. D wished to plead that voluntary intoxication had led him not to realise that the conduct element of the offence – the "allowing" – had taken place. This line of defence was not permitted. It was held that the offence was one of "basic intent", even though "allowing" something to happen would normally be said to contain an implicit element of knowledge or belief that something is happening or has happened.[22]

2.13   The Court of Appeal has since recognised that there is

---

[16]   *Caldwell* [1982] AC 341, 355. The position would appear to be different, however, if the prosecution frames the information or indictment to allege nothing other than that D acted with *intent*. In *Caldwell* it was also held (at p 356) that criminal damage contrary to s 1(2) of the Criminal Damage Act 1971 was an offence of "specific intent" if there was no explicit prosecution allegation of recklessness in respect of the endangerment of life.

[17]   *DPP v Majewski* [1977] AC 443, 476.

[18]   *Savage* [1992] 1 AC 699, 740. Maliciously wounding or inflicting grievous bodily harm, contrary to s 20 of the Offences Against the Person Act 1861, and assault occasioning actual bodily harm, contrary to s 47 of the Offences Against the Person Act 1861, are also offences of basic intent, as is manslaughter.

[19]   Section 22(1) of the Theft Act 1968 requires proof that D knew or believed that the relevant goods were stolen. In *Durante* [1972] 1 WLR 1612, where the Court of Appeal refers to "the necessary intent" rather than the question of knowledge or belief, this state of mind was considered to be a "specific intent".

[20]   "Dishonesty" should be regarded as a "specific intent" because it incorporates a requirement of knowledge (or belief) as to what reasonable people regard as dishonest; see fn 24 in Part 1 above.

[21]   (1994) 158 JP 1138.

[22]   Similarly, in *MacPherson* [1973] RTR 157 it was held that the offence of taking a conveyance without consent or other lawful authority, contrary to s 12(1) of the Theft Act 1968, was one of "basic intent", even though a *purpose* is required for liability (given that the taking must be "for [the taker's] own or another's use").

no universally logical test for distinguishing between crimes in which voluntary intoxication can be advanced as a defence and those in which it cannot; there is a large element of policy; categorisation is achieved on an offence by offence basis.[23]

2.14 What, then, is the underlying policy? We believe that an offence will be regarded as one of "basic intent" if the judiciary conclude that the commission of its external element in a state of voluntary intoxication (without the fault required by the definition of the offence) is the moral equivalent of committing it with the fault required by the definition of the offence, and that D therefore ought to incur criminal liability for the harm or danger caused or created.[24] In other words, the general need to respect definitional requirements of fault can and should be overridden if:

(1) there is no significant moral difference between committing the external element of the offence with its fault element and committing the external element in a self-induced state of intoxication; and

(2) the criminal conviction appropriately labels D as an offender even though, because of D's voluntary consumption of alcohol or some other drug, D acted without the fault required by the definition of the offence.

2.15 The underlying rationale must be that a state of (voluntary) intoxication is liable to make a person do the very things – act indifferently, recklessly or negligently – which the fault element of the offence seeks in its own way to capture. Individuals who commit the external element of any such offence in a self-induced state of intoxication should be made accountable for their actions and any harm caused.

2.16 It follows that, although in *Heard*[25] the Court of Appeal referred to "a large element of policy", in truth this alternative basis for imposing criminal liability fully accords with general legal principle. That is to say, D is incurring criminal liability, and being labelled and punished accordingly, to the extent justified by the blameworthiness of his or her conduct, bearing in mind the need to deter such conduct and provide the public with effective protection.

2.17 It is therefore appropriate to speak of a principle of moral equivalence which permits an intoxicated D to be held liable for an offence of "basic intent" in such circumstances, where D acted without the fault ordinarily required for liability.

---

[23] *Heard* [2007] EWCA Crim 125, [2008] QB 43, para 32, accepting counsel's submission at para 12(ii).

[24] In *Heard* [2007] EWCA Crim 125, [2008] QB 43, para 30(i), the Court of Appeal, referring to *DPP v Majewski* [1977] AC 443, accepted that moral equivalence justified denying D a right to rely on self-induced intoxication if the disputed fault element was not one of "specific intent". See also *Majewski* [1977] AC 443, at p 479, where Lord Simon said that a "mind rendered self-inducedly insensible …, through drink or drugs, to the nature of a prohibited act or to its probable consequences is as wrongful a mind as one which consciously contemplates the prohibited act and foresees its probable consequences (or is reckless as to whether they ensue)".

[25] [2007] EWCA Crim 125, [2008] QB 43.

2.18   The category of "basic intent" offences, as circumscribed by this principle of moral equivalence, includes offences with the fault element usually described as subjective recklessness, a form of advertent wrongdoing. D will be liable for an offence requiring foresight of a risk even though, on account of D's self-induced state of intoxication, D did not in fact foresee that risk (that is, D acted inadvertently). The key to understanding this approach is the view that some types of inadvertent wrongdoing are so blameworthy that they are morally equivalent even to subjective recklessness. In the words of Stephen Gough:

> objectionable drunken conduct is, perhaps because it is so often a matter of thoughtless self-indulgence, one of the more offensive categories of inadvertent wrongdoing.[26]

2.19   But even if one does not accept the argument that inadvertence caused by voluntary intoxication is morally equivalent to advertent recklessness, and therefore one cannot accept that the alternative basis of liability (based on voluntary intoxication) accords with legal principle, the courts' approach may certainly be justified on public policy grounds. D ought to be aware that, by becoming voluntarily intoxicated, D increases the risk that he or she will cause harm to other persons or damage to property. That is enough to justify liability for the range of violent and sexual offences classified as offences of "basic intent".

2.20   The practical consequence of the alternative basis of liability is that any offence requiring a fault element of "recklessness", whether subjective (advertent) or objective (inadvertent), is to be regarded as an offence of "basic intent".[27] Or, to express the matter more accurately, the fault element of recklessness, as the term is generally used, is not to be regarded as a "specific intent".[28]

2.21   For offences of "specific intent", the commission of the external element in a state of voluntary intoxication is *not* equivalent, or sufficiently similar, in moral terms to committing it with the fault element required by the definition of the offence. For this reason the prosecution must prove the required state of mind (that is, the prosecution must prove all facets of the fault element which are "specific intents"). By way of example, the following offences fall within this category of offences:

        (a)   murder (requiring an intention to kill or cause serious harm);[29]

        (b)   theft (requiring an intention permanently to deprive the owner of his or her property);[30] and

---

[26]   S Gough, "Intoxication and Criminal Liability: The Law Commission's Proposed Reforms" (1996) 112 *Law Quarterly Review* 335, p 337.

[27]   *DPP v Majewski* [1977] AC 443, 475 and 479, by Lord Elwyn-Jones LC and Lord Simon respectively; *Caldwell* [1982] AC 341, 355 and 361 to 362, by Lord Diplock and Lord Edmund-Davies (dissenting) respectively.

[28]   We say "generally used" because a complication has arisen as a result of the use of the term in Part 2 of the Serious Crime Act 2007. We address this problem in paras 3.104 to 3.117 below.

[29]   *Sheehan* [1975] 1 WLR 739; *Sooklal v Trinidad and Tobago* [1999] 1 WLR 2011; *McKnight* (2000) *The Times* 5 May.

(c)   handling stolen goods (requiring knowledge or belief that the goods are stolen).[31]

2.22   However, the categorisation of offences as offences of "basic" or "specific" intent is unhelpful for a number of reasons.

2.23   First of all, it is not even possible to categorise some offences until the allegation against D is factually particularised. An example is provided by the offence of sexual assault contrary to section 3 of the Sexual Offences Act 2003. Sexual assault is an offence of "specific intent" if the alleged assault is not by its very nature sexual but is only rendered sexual by D's purpose.[32] Where, however, the assault is unambiguously sexual,[33] and therefore no reference to D's purpose is required, the offence is one of "basic intent".[34]

2.24   It follows that the question should not be whether an offence is to be categorised as one of "specific" or of "basic" intent but whether the offence as charged does or does not require proof of a fault requirement which is classified as a "specific intent". In *Heard*[35] the Court of Appeal rightly accepted that it is necessary to focus on the particular state of mind in issue.[36]

2.25   Secondly, the categorisation of an offence as one of "basic intent" does not begin to explain the approach to be adopted where there is evidence that D was to some extent intoxicated at the material time. If D is charged with having committed an offence of "basic intent", it is sometimes said that the mere fact that D was voluntarily intoxicated at the time he committed the external element provides a sufficient basis for returning a conviction.[37] This cannot be an accurate explanation of the true legal position.

---

[30]   *Ruse v Read* [1949] 1 KB 377; *DPP v Majewski* [1977] AC 443, 477 and 482. It follows that robbery (contrary to s 8(1) of the Theft Act 1968) and burglary with intent to steal (contrary to s 9(1)(a) of the Theft Act 1968) are offences of "specific intent". These offences may also be regarded as "specific intent" offences because of the need to prove dishonesty.

[31]   *Durante* [1972] 1 WLR 1612. This offence may also be regarded as one of "specific intent" because of the need to prove dishonesty.

[32]   See s 78(b) of the Sexual Offences Act 2003 and *R v H* [2005] EWCA Crim 732, [2005] 1 WLR 2005.

[33]   For the purposes of s 78(a) of the 2003 Act.

[34]   This was also the position for indecent assault before the 2003 Act came into force; see *Court* [1989] AC 28 and *C* (1992) 156 JP 649.

[35]   [2007] EWCA Crim 125, [2008] QB 43.

[36]   Above, para 15.

[37]   See, eg, Lord Mustill's view in *Kingston* [1995] 2 AC 355, 369, that self-induced intoxication is "a substitute for the mental element ordinarily required by the offence". See also *DPP v Majewski* [1977] AC 443, 474 to 475:

> If a man of his own volition takes a substance which causes him to cast off the restraints of reason and conscience, no wrong is done to him by holding him answerable criminally for any injury he may do while in that condition. His course of conduct in reducing himself by drugs and drink to that condition in my view supplies the evidence of *mens rea*, of guilty mind certainly sufficient for crimes of basic intent.

2.26   If, for example, D is charged with a "basic intent" offence requiring subjective recklessness, and D was (slightly) intoxicated at the time he or she committed the offence's external element, the court cannot simply hold that proof of (slight) intoxication is enough. D might say that he or she did not foresee the risk required by the concept of subjective recklessness, and contend that his or her lack of foresight was not caused, even in part, by the state of intoxication. In other words, D's defence is that he or she would have acted in the same way with the same state of mind even if he or she had been completely sober.

2.27   Thirdly, the categorisation of an offence as one of "specific intent" or "basic intent" is not related to the level of culpability associated with the commission of the offence. As explained above, rape would still appear to be a "basic intent" offence even though it carries a maximum sentence of life imprisonment. But the offence of maliciously administering a poison (etc) with intent to injure, aggrieve or annoy, which carries a maximum penalty of five years' imprisonment,[38] is without doubt an offence of "specific intent".

2.28   Under the next heading we address in more detail the two approaches adopted by the criminal courts in cases where D was voluntarily intoxicated at the time he or she allegedly committed the external element of an offence.

DETERMINING LIABILITY

Offences of "specific intent" – legal principle and definitional logic

2.29   It is well established that a person charged with an offence of "specific intent" may rely on evidence of self-induced intoxication to avoid liability for that offence. The issue will be whether the jury could conclude that it is reasonably possible that D did not act with the state of mind required by the definition of the offence, and D's intoxicated state may be relevant to the determination of this issue.[39]

2.30   According to the Court of Appeal in *Sheehan*,[40] the jury should be instructed

> to have regard to all the evidence, including that relating to drink,
> to draw such inferences as they think proper from the evidence,
> and on that basis to ask themselves whether they feel sure that
> at the material time the defendant had the requisite intent.[41]

---

[38]   Offences Against the Person Act 1861, s 24.

[39]   *DPP v Beard* [1920] AC 479, 499 and 501 to 502; *DPP v Majewski* [1977] AC 443, 473. In *DPP v Beard* it was said that self-induced intoxication was a defence only if it rendered D *incapable* of forming the necessary "specific intent". However, although the same terminology is still occasionally used (eg, in *Groark* [1999] *Criminal Law Review* 669) it is clear from numerous other cases (eg, *Cole* [1993] *Criminal Law Review* 300, *O'Connor* [1991] *Criminal Law Review* 135, *Garlick* (1980) 72 Cr App R 291, *Pordage* [1975] *Criminal Law Review* 575 and *Sheehan* [1975] 1 WLR 739) that the question for the jury is whether D actually had the required state of mind at the relevant time.

[40]   [1975] 1 WLR 739.

[41]   Above, 744. The point has been repeated in subsequent cases; see, eg, *Davies* [1991] *Criminal Law Review* 469, *Bowden* [1993] *Criminal Law Review* 380 and *Brown* [1998] *Criminal Law Review* 485.

2.31   This accords with an important principle of criminal liability: a person cannot be liable for an offence requiring fault if he or she committed the external element without it. We have already described this approach as one based on "simple definitional logic".[42]

2.32   So, in cases where it is alleged that D committed an offence requiring proof of a culpable state of mind labelled as a "specific intent", the prosecution must always prove that D did indeed act with that state of mind.[43] The only burden on D is evidential.[44] That is to say, there must be credible evidence before the jury that D's state of intoxication was such that he acted without the alleged state of mind.[45]

2.33   This approach accords with the view of a number of academic writers that, as a matter of principle, as well as of definitional logic, D should not be liable for any offence requiring subjective fault if he or she lacked the required state of mind, even if it was because D was voluntarily intoxicated. For example, writing in 1975, Professor Sir John Smith suggested that the House of Lords should:

> recognise that if a particular *mens rea* is an ingredient of an offence, no one can be convicted of that offence if he did not have the *mens rea* in question, whether he was drunk at the time or not.[46]

2.34   This view illustrates what might be called the purists' approach to criminal liability. Purists regard the requirement that the prosecution prove the subjective fault element as a principled rule of the substantive criminal law from which there can be no legitimate derogation.

---

[42]   Paragraph 1.49 above.

[43]   Following *Woolmington* [1935] AC 462, the prosecution must prove the various elements of the offence charged beyond reasonable doubt (unless D makes formal admissions in relation to those elements, obviating the need for proof).

[44]   See, eg, *Sooklal* [1999] 1 WLR 2011 and *McKnight* (2000) *The Times* 5 May.

[45]   The evidence should suggest that D was "rendered so stupid by drink that he [did] not know what he [was] doing" (*A-G for Northern Ireland v Gallagher* [1963] AC 349, 381).

[46]   [1975] *Criminal Law Review* 574.

Offences of "basic intent" – the decision in *DPP v Majewski*

2.35   Notwithstanding the purists' view, the law, in the light of the decision of the House of Lords in *DPP v Majewski*,[47] is that, if D is charged with an offence of "basic intent" requiring subjective fault, and it is proved or admitted that D committed the external element, it is not permissible for the defence to argue that D acted without the required fault on account of self-induced intoxication.[48] Majewski was therefore held to have been properly convicted of the "basic intent" offences of assault occasioning actual bodily harm and assault on a police officer in the execution of his duty even if he had been so intoxicated, following his voluntary consumption of alcohol and other drugs, that he did not know what he was doing.

2.36   According to the House of Lords, D is liable for an offence of "basic intent":

(1)   if D commits its external element without the fault usually required for liability, if the absence of such fault results from self-induced intoxication; or

(2)   if D's self-induced intoxication causes him or her to commit the external element as an automaton.

2.37   Accordingly, there is a rule of substantive law – "the *Majewski* rule" – that D is liable for an offence of subjective recklessness if unaware of the relevant risk by virtue of his or her state of self-induced intoxication.[49] It follows that, if D commits the external element of an offence in a state of self-induced intoxication, thereby causing harm to another person, or another person's death, D will not necessarily escape all criminal liability.

2.38   To give an example, suppose it is proved that D unlawfully killed another person while under the influence of alcohol or some other drug voluntarily taken, but it is reasonably possible that D lacked the intent to kill or cause grievous bodily harm on account of his or her intoxicated state. In such a case, D is not liable for the "specific intent" offence of murder but D *is* liable for the alternative "basic intent" offence of manslaughter.[50] According to Lord Edmund-Davies:

---

[47]   [1977] AC 443.

[48]   The leading speech was delivered by Lord Elwyn-Jones LC, with whom Lords Diplock, Simon and Kilbrandon expressed agreement. Lords Salmon, Edmund-Davies and Russell delivered concurring speeches.

[49]   See para 2.18 above.

[50]   Similarly, if the prosecution charges D with wounding or causing grievous bodily harm with the intent to do grievous bodily harm, contrary to s 18 of the Offences Against the Person Act 1861, but cannot prove that intent because of D's voluntarily intoxicated state at the time the harm was caused, D is nevertheless liable for the alternative "basic intent" offence of maliciously (that is, recklessly) inflicting grievous bodily harm, contrary to s 20 of the Act.

> Illogical though the present law may be, it represents a compromise between the imposition of liability upon inebriates in complete disregard of their condition (on the alleged ground that it was brought on voluntarily), and the total exculpation required by the defendant's actual state of mind at the time he committed the harm in issue.[51]

2.39 Thus, while it is true that D will not be held liable for an offence of "specific intent" if he or she acted without the state of mind required for liability, D will (usually) be liable for an alternative offence of "basic intent" (regardless of the fact that D acted without the state of mind required for that offence).

2.40 As Professor Ashworth points out:

> Murder and wounding with intent are crimes of specific intent, and there is no great loss of social defence in allowing intoxication to negative the intent required for those crimes when the amplitude of the basic intent offences of manslaughter and unlawful wounding lies beneath them – ensuring D's conviction and liability to sentence.[52]

2.41 An example from the case law is provided by *Lipman*,[53] where D killed V by cramming bedclothes into her mouth. D was not liable for the "specific intent" offence of murder as he had killed V in a state of self-induced intoxication, which had led him to believe he was fighting snakes at the centre of the world. However, he was liable for the offence of unlawful and dangerous act manslaughter (because the unlawful act of battery was a "basic intent" offence) for which he received a sentence of six years' imprisonment.

2.42 The *Majewski* rule therefore provides an alternative, objective basis for establishing liability if the offence charged is one of "basic intent". The usual subjective approach is qualified for offences requiring nothing more than recklessness because of the culpable, self-induced reason for D's inadvertence.

Justifying the rule

2.43 The chain of reasoning advanced by the House of Lords in support of the *Majewski* rule may be summarised as follows:

(1) the maintenance of order and the need to keep public and private violence under control is the prime purpose – or one of the prime purposes – of the criminal law;[54]

---

[51] *DPP v Majewski* [1977] AC 443, 495.

[52] Ashworth, *Principles of Criminal Law* (5th ed, 2006) p 212.

[53] [1970] 1 QB 152.

[54] *DPP v Majewski* [1977] AC 443, 469, by Lord Elwyn-Jones LC; by Lord Simon at p 476; by Lord Salmon at p 484; and by Lord Edmund-Davies at p 495.

(2) self-induced intoxication through the consumption of alcohol has been a factor in crimes of violence, such as assault, throughout the history of crime, but in recent decades the problem has become more acute by virtue of the voluntary consumption of other drugs;[55]

(3) to allow D to avoid all liability in a case where he or she has caused injury or death to another person, on the basis that he or she lacked the fault element for liability because of self-induced intoxication, would fail to give effect to the prime purpose of the criminal law; in particular, it would:

    (a) "leave the citizen legally unprotected from unprovoked violence where such violence was the consequence of drink or drugs having obliterated the capacity of the perpetrator to know what he was doing or what were its consequences";[56] and

    (b) "shock the public, ... rightly bring the law into contempt and ... certainly increase one of the really serious menaces facing society today";[57]

(4) to provide the community with sufficient protection, therefore, there must be a "substantive rule of law" to the effect that "self-induced intoxication provides no defence" to an allegation that D committed an offence of "basic intent";[58]

(5) the interests of the accused are adequately protected in that the trial judge or magistrates will, when sentencing, "always carefully [take] into account all the circumstances ... before deciding which of the many courses open should be adopted".[59]

The nature and scope of the rule

2.44 Although the *Majewski* rule means that D can be convicted of an offence requiring subjective recklessness, even though D was not reckless in the way required by the definition, the House of Lords expressed the view that this does not violate the principles of justice. According to Lord Elwyn-Jones:

---

[55] Above, p 469, by Lord Elwyn-Jones LC. See also the comments of Lord Simon at p 476 and Lord Edmund-Davies at p 495.

[56] Above, p 476, by Lord Simon.

[57] Above, p 484, by Lord Salmon. In a similar vein, the Lord Chancellor approved, at p 469, the comments of Lawton LJ in the Court of Appeal as to "how serious from a social and public standpoint the consequences would be if men could behave as [D] did and then claim that they were not guilty of any offence". According to Lord Salmon, at p 484: "the social consequence could be appalling". Lord Russell said, at p 498: "The ordinary citizen who is badly beaten up would rightly think little of the criminal law as an effective protection if, because his attacker had deprived himself of [the] ability to know what he was doing by getting himself drunk or going on a trip with drugs, the attacker is to be held innocent of any crime in the assault."

[58] Above, p 469, by Lord Elwyn-Jones LC. The point that the rule is one of substantive law was also made at p 476.

[59] Above, p 484, by Lord Salmon.

> If a man of his own volition takes a substance which causes him to cast off the restraints of reason and conscience, no wrong is done to him by holding him answerable criminally for any injury he may do while in that condition. His course of conduct in reducing himself by drugs and drink to that condition in my view supplies the evidence of *mens rea*, of guilty mind certainly sufficient for crimes of basic intent.[60]

2.45 The fact of self-induced intoxication does not, however, supply "evidence of *mens rea* ... for crimes of basic intent". Our argument is that, because D voluntarily made himself dangerous in disregard of public safety, that is morally equivalent to having the fault element of recklessness as to others' safety. Consequently D is to be regarded as having acted with a sufficient fault element to warrant a conviction for the offence.

2.46 The legal position may therefore be summarised as follows. The definitional requirements of all criminal offences must be read with the general qualification introduced by the *Majewski* rule for fault elements which are not "specific intents". In particular, if an offence is defined with a requirement of subjective recklessness, it is not always necessary to prove that D acted with that culpable state of mind to secure a conviction. If it is proved or admitted that D committed the external element of such an offence, and at that time D was intoxicated through the voluntary consumption of drink or drugs, liability can be established even though D did not appreciate the relevant risk, so long as it can be proved that D would have appreciated that risk if he or she had been sober.[61]

THE *MAJEWSKI* RULE AND MISTAKES OF FACT

Mistakes of fact and "basic intent" offences

2.47 Where D is charged with an offence of "basic intent", the *Majewski* rule applies to mistakes of present fact as much as it applies to mistakes relating to future possibilities. This is the case whether the mistake relates to an element of fault or to a potential defence on which D might wish to rely.

---

[60] Above, pp 474 to 475.

[61] Compare *Smith & Hogan, Criminal Law* (12th ed, 2008) p 298 which, we suggest, oversimplifies the true position:

> There is ... an implied qualification to every statute creating an offence and specifying a *mens rea* other than a specific intent. The *mens rea* must be proved – except ... where the accused was intoxicated through the voluntary taking of drink or drugs.

2.48   For example, before section 1 of the Sexual Offences Act 2003 came into force, D would be liable for rape even if, by virtue of his self-induced intoxicated state, he did not know, and was not aware of the possibility, that the complainant (V) was not consenting. The culpable state of mind for rape was that D "knows that [V] does not consent to the intercourse or is reckless as to whether [V] consents to it".[62] Rape so defined was regarded as an offence of "basic intent", so even a genuine mistake as to V's state of mind could not allow D to avoid liability for his conduct, if that mistake was caused by self-induced intoxication alone.[63]

2.49   Section 1(1)(c) of the Sexual Offences Act 2003 now provides that, for D to be liable for rape, it is enough that he "does not reasonably believe that [V] consents". D's self-induced intoxicated state is therefore to be disregarded by the jury when determining whether he is liable for rape, because reasonable grounds for a belief are grounds which would be reasonable to a sober man.[64]

2.50   The analysis applied to the fault element in "basic intent" offences such as rape also applies when D acts under a mistake as to an element of self-defence.

2.51   As a general rule, if D raises the defence of self-defence, he or she is entitled to be judged according to the factual circumstances which D perceived, even if D was mistaken about the circumstances and the mistake was one a reasonable person would not have made.[65] This general rule does not apply, however, if D's mistaken understanding of the facts resulted from a self-induced state of intoxication. In other words, an unreasonable but genuine mistake of fact arising from self-induced intoxication cannot be relied on where self-defence is raised in respect of an allegation that D committed an offence of "basic intent".[66]

2.52   Thus, if D's drinking leads him mistakenly to believe that V is about to launch an attack on him, D will not be able to rely on the mistake to support a defence of self-defence if it is alleged that D committed an offence of "basic intent". Examples of such offences are common assault and assault occasioning actual bodily harm.

---

[62]   Sexual Offences Act 1956, s 1(2)(b).

[63]   That rape was to be regarded as an offence of "basic intent" – and that D's mistaken belief, caused by self-induced intoxication, that V was consenting was irrelevant – is apparent from the speech of Lord Russell in *DPP v Majewski* [1977] AC 443, 499 to 500 and the subsequent decision of the Court of Appeal in *Woods* (1981) 74 Cr App R 312. See also *Fotheringham* (1988) 88 Cr App R 206, where the Court of Appeal held that D's mistaken belief, caused by self-induced intoxication, that V was his wife was no defence to the allegation of rape (as then defined).

[64]   As explained in para 2.9 above, the use of the word "intentionally" in s 1(1)(a) of the Sexual Offences Act 2003 has not affected the status of rape as an offence of "basic intent".

[65]   *Williams (Gladstone)* (1983) 78 Cr App R 276, 280; *Beckford* [1988] AC 130, 144.

[66]   *O'Grady* [1987] QB 995; *Hatton* [2005] EWCA Crim 2951, [2006] 1 Cr App R 16 (247). See also the discussion in J Rogers, "Have-A-Go Heroes" (2008) 158 *New Law Journal*, Feb 29, 318.

2.53 In similar fashion, a mistake as to the facts caused by self-induced intoxication cannot be relied on in support of any defence which requires reference to the state of mind of a reasonable (and therefore sober) person, such as the defence of duress.[67]

Mistakes of fact and "specific intent" offences

2.54 In *Hatton*,[68] a recent case of alleged murder, a severely-intoxicated D battered V to death with a sledgehammer and raised self-defence on the basis that he must have believed that V was attacking him. The Court of Appeal confirmed that the rule on mistakes of fact relating to self-defence for "basic intent" offences[69] also applies to offences of "specific intent". The Court also reaffirmed the rule that, although mistaken facts relied on in support of a claim to self-defence do not ordinarily need to be reasonable,[70] mistakes caused by voluntary intoxication cannot be relied on.

2.55 Thus, in a case of alleged murder D may rely on evidence of self-induced intoxication to show that he or she did not act with the required "specific intent" (to kill or cause grievous bodily harm to another person). However, D cannot rely on such evidence to show that he or she was mistaken as to the factual circumstances relevant to the claim that D believed he or she faced an attack by the deceased.

2.56 Giving the judgment of the Court of Appeal, Lord Phillips CJ relied on what was said by Lord Lane CJ in the earlier case of *O'Grady*[71] to justify this rule:

> This brings us to the question of public order. There are two competing interests. On the one hand the interest of the defendant who has only acted according to what he believed to be necessary to protect himself, and on the other hand that of the public in general and the victim in particular who, probably through no fault of his own, has been injured or perhaps killed because of the defendant's drunken mistake. Reason recoils from the conclusion that in such circumstances a defendant is entitled to leave the Court without a stain on his character.[72]

2.57 In broad terms, the "competing interests" to which Lord Lane referred are the same interests which were balanced by the House of Lords in *DPP v Majewski*[73] when considering whether to permit D to deny the fault element of a "basic intent" offence which he or she would have had if sober. There are really three interests:

---

[67] For a summary of the present law on duress, see: Murder, Manslaughter and Infanticide, Law Com No 304 (2006) pp 112 to 114.

[68] [2005] EWCA Crim 2951, [2006] 1 Cr App R 16 (247).

[69] Paragraphs 2.50 to 2.52 above.

[70] *Williams (Gladstone)* (1983) 78 Cr App R 276, 280; *Beckford* [1988] AC 130, 144.

[71] [1987] QB 995, followed in *O'Connor* [1991] *Criminal Law Review* 135.

[72] [1987] QB 995, 1000, by Lord Lane CJ, cited in *Hatton* [2005] EWCA Crim 2951, [2006] 1 Cr App R 16 (247), at para 13.

[73] [1977] AC 443.

(1)   the need to respect requirements of fault;

(2)   the need to protect the public from drunken violence; and

(3)   the need to label appropriately those who violate personal and property rights (bearing in mind the reason for the violation).

2.58   In *DPP v Majewski*[74] the House of Lords decided to strike the balance between the competing interests in favour of protecting the public, and the Court of Appeal has done so again in *Hatton*,[75] following *O'Grady*[76] and *O'Connor*.[77]

2.59   Lord Lane's rationale is open to criticism, however, as the Court of Appeal itself acknowledged in *Hatton*.[78] If the case is one of alleged murder and D were to be permitted to rely on an unreasonable mistake of fact in support of self-defence, and that defence was successful, D's mistake would provide no defence to the alternative "basic intent" offence of manslaughter. The latter offence is governed by the *Majewski* rule,[79] so D would not leave the court "without a stain on his character". Be that as it may, the Court of Appeal in *Hatton*[80] considered itself to be bound by *O'Grady*,[81] suggesting only that the question whether or not the law is soundly based "must be decided elsewhere".[82]

2.60   Parliament has decided that this rule is indeed soundly based and has recently enacted legislation to codify it. Section 76 of the Criminal Justice and Immigration Act 2008, which is intended to clarify the law on the use of reasonable force in self-defence,[83] provides in subsection (4)(b) that, where self-defence is relied on, D may rely on a mistaken belief as to the circumstances whether or not the mistake was a reasonable one to have made. However, this is qualified by subsection (5) which provides that "subsection (4)(b) does not enable D to rely on any mistaken belief attributable to intoxication that was voluntarily induced".

---

[74]   Above.

[75]   [2005] EWCA Crim 2951, [2006] 1 Cr App R 16 (247).

[76]   [1987] QB 995.

[77]   [1991] *Criminal Law Review* 135.

[78]   [2005] EWCA Crim 2951, [2006] 1 Cr App R 16 (247), paras 23 and 25.

[79]   Manslaughter, whether by gross negligence or an unlawful and dangerous (criminal) act, is a "basic intent" offence. However, it might be argued that a conviction for manslaughter would be insufficient in cases of this sort to satisfy the demands of retribution, labelling and public protection.

[80]   [2005] EWCA Crim 2951, [2006] 1 Cr App R 16 (247), paras 23 and 24.

[81]   [1987] QB 995.

[82]   [2005] EWCA Crim 2951, [2006] 1 Cr App R 16 (247), para 26.

[83]   And the equivalent rule for the analogous defence in section 3(1) of the Criminal Law Act 1967.

2.61   In Part 3 of this Report[84] we explain why we agree with the Government's approach in this respect and set out our principled reasons for rejecting the contrary argument, based on the non-applicability of the *Majewski* rule to "specific intents", that there should be a special rule for cases of self-defence if D is charged with an offence of "specific intent".

2.62   With regard to the partial defences to murder, the old case of *Letenock*[85] provides some support for the view that D may rely on a mistake as to the facts caused by voluntary intoxication if D is running the defence of provocation. It would be surprising if this ever was or is still the law, particularly as it would run contrary to the approach adopted by the Court of Appeal in *O'Grady*[86] and *Hatton*,[87] and could give rise to difficulties if self-defence and provocation are run together as alternative defences.

DIRECTING THE JURY IN ACCORDANCE WITH THE *MAJEWSKI* RULE

2.63   Returning to offences of "basic intent", the *Majewski* rule would appear to apply whatever the degree of intoxication, so long as it "prevented D from foreseeing ... what he would have foreseen ... had he been sober".[88] But what of the situation where an intoxicated D was not subjectively reckless (as required by the substantive offence) for a reason other than his or her intoxication, or because of intoxication in tandem with one or more other factors?

2.64   Logically, in a case where D is charged with an offence of "basic intent" and D claims not to have had the (subjective) fault ordinarily required for liability, the jury should be directed in the following terms:

(1)   if D's self-induced intoxication of itself caused D not to have the state of mind required for liability, and D would have had that state of mind if sober, the jury should for that reason return a verdict of guilty;[89]

(2)   if D's self-induced intoxication was one of two or more factors which caused, or might have caused, D not to have the state of mind required for liability, the jury should consider whether D would have had the required state of mind if D had not at that time been intoxicated.[90] So, if we take the fault requirement of subjective recklessness:

(a)   if D *would* have been aware of the relevant risk, if D had not been intoxicated to that extent, D is to be held liable for the offence;

---

[84]   Paragraphs 3.53 to 3.72.

[85]   (1917) 12 Cr App R 221.

[86]   [1987] QB 995.

[87]   [2005] EWCA Crim 2951, [2006] 1 Cr App R 16 (247).

[88]   *Smith & Hogan, Criminal Law* (12th ed, 2008) p 299.

[89]   The same approach applies if self-induced intoxication caused D to act as an automaton, as in *DPP v Majewski* [1977] AC 443 (alcohol) and *Lipman* [1970] 1 QB 152 (LSD).

[90]   Williams, *Textbook of Criminal Law* (2nd ed, 1983) p 475 rightly points out that the "law can hardly be that evidence . . . that the defendant had consumed a couple of pints of beer turns what would otherwise have been an offence requiring [fault element] into an offence of strict liability".

(b)   if it is reasonably possible that D *would not* have been aware of the relevant risk, even if D had not been intoxicated, D is not to be held liable for the offence.[91]

2.65   Support for this interpretation of the law can be found in the leading speech of Lord Elwyn-Jones LC in *DPP v Majewski*,[92] to the effect that the *Majewski* rule "is in line with the American Model Penal Code (s 2.08(2))",[93] which provides as follows:

> When recklessness establishes an element of the offence, if the actor, due to self-induced intoxication, is unaware of a risk of which he would have been aware had he been sober, such unawareness is immaterial.

2.66   Lord Diplock, who gave the leading speech in the subsequent case of *Caldwell*,[94] provided the following interpretation of what was said by Lord Elwyn-Jones:

> The Lord Chancellor accepted at p 475 as correctly stating English law the provision in section 2.08(2) of the American Model Penal Code.

2.67   In *Richardson*,[95] a case concerning the "basic intent" offence of inflicting grievous bodily harm contrary to section 20 of the Offences Against the Person Act 1861 (which requires foresight on the part of D of harm being caused by his or her conduct)[96] the Court of Appeal held that the question for the jury comprises two alternatives, namely:

(1)   whether D actually foresaw the possibility of some harm being caused to V; and, if not,

(2)   whether D would have foreseen, had D not been drinking alcohol, that his or her conduct might cause V some harm.[97]

2.68   The same approach is evident in section 6(5) of the Public Order Act 1986, which provides that, for the purposes of section 6, "a person whose awareness is impaired by [self-induced] intoxication shall be taken to be aware of that of which he would be aware if not intoxicated ... ."

---

[91]   In the words of Professor Glanville Williams, "Two Nocturnal Blunders "(1990) 140 *New Law Journal* 1564: "the defendant will still get off if the court thinks that a sober person might have made the same mistake".

[92]   [1977] AC 443.

[93]   Above, p 475.

[94]   [1982] AC 341.

[95]   [1999] 1 Cr App R 392.

[96]   *Savage* [1992] 1 AC 699, 751.

[97]   [1999] 1 Cr App R 392 at p 396, following the decision of the Courts-Martial Appeal Court in *Aitken* [1992] 1 WLR 1006, 1011 to 1017. Surprisingly, however, the Court of Appeal felt (at p 397) that an honest mistake as to whether V was *consenting* to D's conduct was a defence, even if D would have known that V was not consenting if he had not been intoxicated. We consider this aspect of the decision to be incorrect, given the approach adopted by the Court of Appeal in relation to D's mistaken understanding of consent in cases of alleged rape and indecent assault.

2.69   Suppose a drunken D throws an empty beer bottle across a public bar to see it smash into the wall, but it hits and injures another customer. The relevant offence under section 20 of the Offences Against the Person Act 1861 requires subjective recklessness as to whether harm might be caused, and hence it is an offence of "basic intent". Accordingly, D is guilty even if he or she did not have that state of mind, so long as the jury is satisfied that D would have had it if he or she had been sober. The fact that D did not foresee the risk that a customer might be hit by the bottle and injured will provide D with no defence to a charge of recklessly inflicting grievous bodily harm.

2.70   This is a straightforward example. We accept that other hypothetical situations may not be so easy for a jury or bench of magistrates to resolve, particularly if "there is more than one plausible reason adduced for inadvertence to risk: for example, tiredness, innate ... irascibility, low intelligence and so on".[98]

NO-FAULT OFFENCES AND OFFENCES REQUIRING OBJECTIVE FAULT

2.71   If D is charged with having committed an offence requiring no element of fault, the fact that D was acting in a state of self-induced intoxication is of no relevance to his or her liability for that offence.

2.72   Similarly, if D is charged with having committed an offence of negligence while intoxicated, D may be liable (without reference to the *Majewski* rule) simply because his or her conduct falls below the standard to be expected of a reasonably competent, sober person in D's position.

2.73   If D is charged with having committed an offence requiring proof of objective recklessness, in line with the test established in *Caldwell*,[99] then:

(1)   if, on account of his or her voluntary intoxication, D gave no thought to the existence of the relevant risk, but a reasonable, sober person would have foreseen that risk, D is *Caldwell* reckless and therefore liable;[100]

(2)   if D relies on the "lacuna" to the *Caldwell* test, that is, D says that he or she consciously considered whether the risk existed and decided that there was no risk at all, then liability is established (by virtue of the *Majewski* rule for recklessness) if D *would* have foreseen the risk had he or she not been voluntarily intoxicated.

2.74   If D is charged with an offence of no fault, or an offence requiring proof of objective fault, and D is able to run a general defence based on a mistaken understanding of the factual circumstances, then the court will apply the general principles set out above for such defences.[101]

---

[98] E Paton, "Reformulating the Intoxication Rules: The Law Commission's Report" [1995] *Criminal Law Review* 382, 383.

[99] [1982] AC 341; see para 1.12(7) above.

[100] Compare *Cullen* [1993] *Criminal Law Review* 936, where this was overlooked.

[101] Paragraphs 2.50 to 2.53.

INVOLUNTARY INTOXICATION

The general position

2.75 In a case where it is proved that D committed the external element of the offence charged, but D lacked the required fault for liability on account of having been involuntarily intoxicated, D is not liable for that offence. This is the case whether the offence charged, an offence requiring proof of fault, is one of "specific intent" or "basic intent".[102]

2.76 For example, suppose that D's orange juice has been surreptitiously laced with alcohol or a drug. Having consumed the drink, D throws a brick at V without any appreciation of the risk that V would thereby apprehend or experience an impact. D would not be liable for common assault or battery; nor would D be liable for unlawful and dangerous act manslaughter should V be killed by the brick. The absence of subjective recklessness would prevent D from incurring liability for those "basic intent" offences. It goes without saying that the absence of the intention to cause serious harm or death would prevent D from being liable for the "specific intent" offences of causing grievous bodily harm with intent or murder.[103]

2.77 In cases of this sort D would not have acted with the subjective fault element for the offence in question and, crucially, would not be responsible for bringing about the intoxicated state which prevented him or her from having the fault element. So, where D's intoxication has been brought about involuntarily, there can be no justification for overturning the general principle that, for liability, D must act with the fault required by the definition of the offence charged. This was accepted in *Kingston*,[104] where Lord Mustill said:

> once the involuntary nature of the intoxication is added the ... theories of *Majewski* fall away, and the position reverts to what it would have been if *Majewski* ... had not been decided, namely that the offence is not made out ...[105]

---

[102] *Kingston* [1995] 2 AC 355, 370. See also *Smith & Hogan, Criminal Law* (12th ed, 2008) p 296 and Williams, *Textbook of Criminal Law* (2nd ed, 1983) p 482. Section 6(5) of the Public Order Act 1986 provides as follows (emphasis added): "For the purposes of this section a person whose awareness is impaired by intoxication shall be taken to be aware of that of which he would be aware if not intoxicated, *unless he shows . . . that his intoxication was not self-induced.*"

[103] If D's own alcoholic drink was laced, the effect of the additional alcohol or drugs would presumably be regarded as involuntary intoxication, assuming it would be possible in practice to distinguish between the effects of the different intoxicants.

[104] [1995] 2 AC 355.

[105] Above, p 370. What Lord Mustill says about the pre-*Majewski* law may be inaccurate, in that broadly the same approach as that taken in *Majewski* had previously been taken in *Beard* [1920] AC 479.

2.78 Similarly, if involuntary intoxication caused D to act in a state of automatism, D may rely on the defence of (non-insane) automatism in respect of any offence requiring volition.[106] This defence is generally available so long as the state of automatism was caused by an external agent and not culpably self-induced.[107]

2.79 The situation where D's drink or food has been surreptitiously laced with a drug, or D has been physically restrained and the intoxicant forcibly administered, are obvious examples of involuntary intoxication. No doubt the taking of drugs following a threat of serious harm would be regarded the same way, by analogy with the defence of duress.

2.80 One situation which has been addressed by the courts, and has been held to be a form of involuntary intoxication outside the scope of the *Majewski* rule, is where D has intentionally but faultlessly brought about his or her own intoxicated state. An example would be where D has taken a drug in good faith for a medical purpose in accordance with his or her doctor's advice. This particular aspect of involuntary intoxication, which may also raise the issue of automatism, is addressed below.

Intoxication which is self-induced but involuntary

2.81 In *Bailey*[108] D (a diabetic) said that he caused V's grievous bodily harm whilst in a state of self-induced automatism occasioned by his having taken insufficient food after a dose of insulin. He therefore claimed that he should not be liable for the "specific intent" offence of causing grievous bodily harm with the intent to do grievous bodily harm, contrary to section 18 of the Offences Against the Person Act 1861, or for the "basic intent" offence of inflicting grievous bodily harm, contrary to section 20 of the same Act. The Court of Appeal came to the following conclusion as to the scope of the defence of automatism:

> [S]elf-induced automatism, other than due to intoxication from alcohol or drugs, may provide a defence to crimes of basic intent. The question in each case will be whether the prosecution have proved the necessary element of recklessness.[109]

2.82 The word "recklessness" was used by the Court of Appeal to refer to the fault required of D in bringing about the condition of automatism. To be liable for an offence requiring subjective recklessness, it seems D would need to have been subjectively reckless, at least, in bringing about his or her condition:

---

[106] The Scottish case of *Ross v HM Advocate* 1991 SLT 564, where D's can of lager was laced with LSD and Temazepam causing him to act as a violent automaton, provides an example of the type of situation.

[107] *Burns* (1973) 58 Cr App R 364; *Quick* [1973] QB 910; *Bailey* [1983] 1 WLR 760.

[108] [1983] 1 WLR 760.

[109] Above, p 765. Self-induced automatism was already established as a defence to offences of "specific intent", insofar as the state of automatism meant that D did not act with the culpable state of mind required for liability. In *Bailey* D was convicted of the s 18 offence and the jury was not required to return a verdict on the alternative s 20 offence. D appealed against his conviction for the s 18 offence on the basis that the jury had been misdirected. His appeal was dismissed on the ground that there was insufficient evidence that he had acted in a state of automatism.

> In cases of assault, if the accused knows that his actions or inaction are likely to make him aggressive, unpredictable or uncontrolled with the result that he may cause some injury to others and he persists in the action or takes no remedial action when he knows it is required, it will be open to the jury to find that he was reckless.[110]

2.83 Accordingly, D may rely on the defence of automatism if charged with an offence of "basic intent", even if the automatism was self-induced, so long as D was not at fault in bringing about that state. It seems that D will be at fault, and therefore unable to rely on the defence, only if he or she is aware of the "likelihood" of acting in the way which forms the basis of the allegation.[111]

2.84 The decision in *Bailey*[112] does not detract from the *Majewski* rule that, generally, self-induced intoxication by alcohol or other drugs cannot negative fault if the offence is one of "basic intent"; but the case has been relied on to limit the scope of the *Majewski* rule for such offences.

2.85 In *Hardie*,[113] which concerned an allegation of aggravated criminal damage by arson,[114] it was not in dispute that D had started the fire. However, D claimed that he was intoxicated on account of his having consumed a large quantity of his former partner's old stock of Valium to ease his distressed state following the breakdown of their relationship. The Court of Appeal concluded that the *Majewski* rule does not apply if the drug taken is "wholly different in kind from drugs which are liable to cause unpredictability or aggressiveness", even if the drug was not taken on medical prescription.[115] Accordingly, it was held that the trial judge should have directed the jury to consider, first, whether D's consumption of Valium meant that he had been unable to appreciate the risks to property and persons from his actions and, if so, secondly, whether he had been "reckless" in taking the Valium.

---

[110] Above, p 765.

[111] Compare *Quick* [1973] 1 QB 910, 922 (emphasis added): "A self-induced incapacity will not excuse . . . , nor will one which could have been *reasonably foreseen* as a result of either doing, or omitting to do something, as, for example, . . . failing to have regular meals while taking insulin." According to this objective test, D will be regarded as having been voluntarily intoxicated if it was reasonably foreseeable that his or her act or omission would lead to intoxication.

[112] [1983] 1 WLR 760.

[113] [1985] 1 WLR 64.

[114] Section 1(2)–(3) of the Criminal Damage Act 1971.

[115] [1985] 1 WLR 64, p 70. It was recognised, however, that this exception may itself be subject to exceptions: "It may well be that the taking of a sedative or soporific drug will, in certain circumstances, be no answer, for example in a case of reckless driving ..."

2.86   The position would therefore appear to be that if D was intoxicated as a result of voluntarily taking a certain quantity of a sedative or soporific drug, the *Majewski* rule for self-induced intoxication will apply only if D was reckless in taking that drug in that quantity. The court intimated that "recklessness" in this context means that "it was known to [D] or even generally known that the taking of Valium in the quantity taken would be liable to render a person aggressive or incapable of appreciating risks to others or have other [analogous] side effects".[116] Insofar as the Court of Appeal envisaged an alternative, objective form of recklessness – which is not clear from the judgment – it may have been because an objective test was then sufficient for liability for criminal damage.[117]

2.87   Nevertheless, the principle which can be drawn from *Hardie*[118] would now appear to be established. Faultless self-induced intoxication by drugs is to be regarded as involuntary intoxication, and therefore outside the scope of the *Majewski* rule.

2.88   One type of faultless self-induced intoxication is intoxication caused by the consumption of prescribed drugs in accordance with properly taken medical advice. This is implicit in the decision of the Court of Appeal in *Hardie*.[119] It was also thought to be the law in *Quick*,[120] a case of assault occasioning actual bodily harm where D, a diabetic, claimed to have acted as an automaton on account of hypoglycaemia (through taking insufficient food after a dose of insulin) and alcohol. The Court of Appeal accepted that D's "alleged mental condition ... was not caused by his diabetes but by his use of the insulin prescribed by his doctor" and concluded that:[121]

> [D] was entitled to have his defence of automatism left to the jury ... If he was in a confused mental condition, was it due to a hypoglycaemic episode or to too much alcohol? If the former, to what extent had he brought about his condition by not following his doctor's instructions about taking regular meals? Did he know that he was getting into a hypoglycaemic state? If yes, why did he not use the antidote of eating a lump of sugar as he had been advised to do?[122]

---

[116] Above, p 69.

[117] *Caldwell* [1982] AC 341, now superseded by *G* [2003] UKHL 50, [2004] 1 AC 1034. *Quick* [1973] 1 QB 910 (fn 111 above) also suggests that an objective test suffices.

[118] [1985] 1 WLR 64.

[119] [1985] 1 WLR 64, 70: "It is true that Valium is a drug and it is true that it was taken deliberately and not taken on medical prescription, but the drug is, in our view, wholly different in kind from drugs which are liable to cause unpredictability or aggressiveness."

[120] [1973] QB 910.

[121] Above, pp 922 to 923.

[122] This is a subjective test for fault. However, as pointed out already (fn 111) the Court propounded a test of *reasonable* foresight at p 922.

2.89   Faultless self-induced intoxication, as a species of involuntary intoxication, falls outside the scope of the *Majewski* doctrine. As explained above,[123] in any case of involuntary intoxication D can liable for an offence of "basic intent" requiring proof of subjective fault only if he or she acted with the culpable state of mind actually required by the definition of the offence.

VOLUNTARY INTOXICATION AND INSANITY[124]

2.90   If D's use of alcohol or other drugs results in a condition amounting to a "disease of the mind"[125] affecting his or her ability to reason at the time the external element of the offence was committed, D may plead the defence of insanity.[126] D does not need to have been intoxicated at the time he or she committed the external element of the offence to be able to rely on the defence of insanity, where D's insanity was caused by intoxication.[127]

2.91   By contrast, if D is a psychopath who, though generally "normal", is likely to have an explosive outburst when intoxicated because of his or her reduced level of self-control, the defence of insanity cannot be relied on to avoid liability.[128]

2.92   If D was intoxicated at the time he or she committed the external element of the offence charged, it will be necessary for the court to determine whether D's misunderstanding of his or her conduct was caused by the intoxicant or by the defect of reason arising from the (possibly temporary) disease of the mind. If it was the disease of the mind, D may be entitled to an acquittal on the ground of insanity. If it was the intoxicant, D may be liable for an offence of "basic intent" if he or she lacked the "specific intent" for a related offence.

---

[123] Paragraphs 2.75 to 2.77.

[124] For the law on intoxication and diminished responsibility as a partial defence to murder, see: Partial Defences to Murder, Law Commission Consultation Paper No 173 (2003), pp 149 to 154 (and, most recently, *Wood* [2008] EWCA Crim 1305). This aspect of the law is beyond the scope of this Report and our general recommendations for intoxication and criminal liability.

[125] For example, delirium tremens.

[126] The issue of insanity is determined by reference to the *M'Naghten* Rules, taken from *M'Naghten's Case* (1843) 10 Cl & Fin 200. See: *DPP v Beard* [1920] AC 479, 500 to 501; *A-G for Northern Ireland v Gallagher* [1963] AC 349, 375 and 381; and *Kingston* [1995] 2 AC 355, 369.

[127] See, for example, *Davis* (1881) 14 Cox CC 563.

[128] *A-G for Northern Ireland v Gallagher* [1963] AC 349.

2.93 In *Burns*,[129] a case of alleged indecent assault, it was apparently the cumulative effect of brain damage, medication (taken, it seems, otherwise than on medical advice) and alcohol that led to D's state of intoxication. The Court of Appeal opined that D would have been entitled to an acquittal on the basis of (non-insane) automatism if he might have been in an automatous condition caused at least partly by the medication and alcohol. This was despite the risk of repetition and notwithstanding the fact that D was charged with a sexual offence of "basic intent".[130] The decision can be explained only on the basis that it was an application of the principle, subsequently established in *Hardie*,[131] that D was not "reckless" in taking the "non-dangerous" medication with alcohol and his intoxication was therefore involuntary.

VOLUNTARY INTOXICATION AND "HONEST BELIEF" PROVISIONS

2.94 In *Jaggard v Dickinson*,[132] an intoxicated D damaged property in the mistaken belief that it belonged to a person who would have consented to the damage. The Divisional Court held that where D is charged under section 1(1) of the Criminal Damage Act 1971,[133] the *Majewski* rule on self-induced intoxication does not apply to the statutory defence of lawful excuse set out in section 5(2) of the Act.

2.95 This is a troubling judgment for two reasons. First, the offence itself is one of "basic intent". Secondly, the general position for defences which allow D to rely on a mistaken understanding of the circumstances is that a mistake induced by voluntary intoxication cannot be relied on (even if other unreasonable mistakes can be relied on).[134]

---

[129] (1973) 58 Cr App R 364.

[130] Compare *Stripp* (1978) 69 Cr App R 318, a case involving a number of alleged motoring offences. In that case it was said that if D's automatous state might have been caused by concussion (from a blow to the head) rather than by D's state of self-induced intoxication, D would be entitled to rely on the defence of (non-insane) automatism.

[131] [1985] 1 WLR 64.

[132] [1981] 1 QB 527.

[133] It is an offence under s 1(1) to destroy or damage property belonging to another person.

[134] See paras 2.50 to 2.53 above. Accordingly, Parliament presumably intended that the *Majewski* rule's almost identical predecessor, the rule in *DPP v Beard* [1920] AC 479, would apply to the defence in s 5(2) of the 1971 Act.

2.96   The reason given by the Divisional Court for its decision in *Jaggard v Dickinson*[135] was that section 5 expressly states that nothing more is required than an honest belief.[136] It was therefore irrelevant whether D's mistaken belief arose from a state of self-induced intoxication or indeed any other (unreasonable) cause. The evidence of self-induced intoxication actually supported D's defence, as it "lent colour to her evidence about the state of her belief".[137]

2.97   In a case of alleged criminal damage, D may therefore rely on his or her intoxicated state, and thereby avoid liability, by showing that he or she made a genuine mistake in respect of the owner's consent. Of course, if D's defence is that D mistakenly believed that he or she was damaging his or her *own* property, because of an intoxicated state, D is liable for criminal damage.[138] As explained already, the offence under section 1(1) is one of "basic intent", so there can be no defence of honestly mistaking another person's property for one's own if that mistake was caused by self-induced intoxication.[139]

VOLUNTARY INTOXICATION AND SECONDARY LIABILITY

2.98   It is now well established that, in a case where D does not actually perpetrate the commission of an offence of "specific intent" (such as murder), but provides the perpetrator (P) of that offence with encouragement or assistance in the context of a joint criminal enterprise to commit a different offence (such as burglary), D will be liable for the offence of "specific intent" (that is, the murder) if D foresaw the possibility that it might be committed during the course of the joint enterprise.[140]

2.99   Although the state of mind required for secondary liability in such a case – what might be called the "*Chan Wing Siu* state of mind"[141] – is superficially similar to the concept of subjective recklessness, it is conceptually different.

---

[135] [1981] 1 QB 527.

[136] D relied on s 5(2)(a), which provides a defence if D "believed that the person or persons whom he believed to be entitled to consent to the destruction of or damage to the property in question had so consented, or would have so consented ... ". Section 5(3) provides that, for the purposes of s 5, "it is immaterial whether a belief is justified or not if it is honestly held".

[137] [1981] 1 QB 527, 531. Compare *Gannon* (1987) 87 Cr App R 254, regarding the "belief that he has lawful authority" defence in s 12(6) of the Theft Act 1968 to a charge of taking a conveyance without consent under s 12(1). The Court of Appeal held that D's drunken state was not evidence tending to show he had the exculpatory belief; so, as D had not been able to discharge his evidential burden, the issue should not have been addressed by the trial judge. The Court of Appeal did, however, expressly leave open the question whether a drunken belief could satisfy the s 12(6) defence.

[138] See *Smith* [1974] QB 354.

[139] In the words of *Smith & Hogan, Criminal Law* (12th ed, 2008) p 307: "If D, being drunk, destroys X's property believing that it is the property of Y who would consent to his doing so, this is a defence; but if he destroys X's property believing that it is his own, it is not."

[140] *Chan Wing-Siu* [1985] 1 AC 168, *Powell and Daniels* [1999] 1 AC 1.

[141] From *Chan Wing-Siu* [1985] 1 AC 168.

2.100   The concept of subjective recklessness evolved in the context of, and has traditionally been regarded as concerned with, the unjustifiable taking of a contemplated risk by D in relation to D's *own* hazardous conduct. The *Chan Wing Siu* state of mind, by contrast, is the foresight of a possibility that a criminal offence will be committed by another party to a joint criminal enterprise. It is not a form of "recklessness" as the concept has traditionally been understood. For this reason, it could, indeed should, be regarded as a form of "specific intent" if there is also a "specific intent" required by the definition of the offence committed by P (which D must foresee).

2.101   But even if the *Chan Wing Siu* state of mind could be regarded as a form of subjective "recklessness", it is doubtful whether the courts would regard it as such. To regard the *Chan Wing Siu* state of mind as a species of recklessness would extend the doctrine of joint enterprise so as to permit D to be liable for a murder committed by P on the basis that, although D did not actually foresee the possibility of murder being committed (because D was voluntarily intoxicated), D *would* have foreseen the possibility if he or she had been sober. Given the seriousness of the offence (and the mandatory life sentence which follows a conviction for it) it is difficult to envisage that the courts would be willing to convict D of murder on this basis.[142] That would be an unacceptable application of the "absolutist" principle criticised earlier.[143]

VOLUNTARY INTOXICATION AND INCHOATE ASSISTING / ENCOURAGING

2.102   We address the position for inchoate liability under Part 2 of the Serious Crime Act 2007[144] in some detail in Part 3 of this Report.

2.103   For present purposes it suffices to explain that Part 2 of the Act includes, amongst other things, a test for determining the liability of a person (D) who assists or encourages another person (P) to commit a prospective offence ("crime X"), whether or not crime X is committed, based on D's being "reckless" as to:

(1)   P's fault;

(2)   the consequence requirement of crime X, if any; and

(3)   the circumstance requirement of crime X, if any.[145]

2.104   The use of the term "reckless" in the 2007 Act means that the state of mind (on the part of D) to which the term refers could be construed as a form of fault covered by the *Majewski* rule, even if crime X has been defined with a fault requirement of "specific intent".

---

[142] It is to be noted that the trial judge's summing up in *English* [1999] 1 AC 1 (p 27) suggests that the jury were directed to take D's intoxicated state of mind into account as a factor bearing on his secondary liability for murder, indicating that some judges at least already regard this state of mind as a "specific intent" if it relates to an offence of "specific intent".

[143] See para 1.56 above.

[144] The relevant provisions came into force on 1 October 2008; see The Serious Crime Act 2007 (Commencement No 3) Order 2008 (SI 2008 No 2504).

[145] See s 47(5)(a)(ii) and (b)(ii).

2.105 If the term "reckless" in Part 2 of the 2007 Act is so construed, it follows by analogy that there would be a greater risk that the *Chan Wing Siu* state of mind would also be construed as a form of subjective "recklessness" covered by the *Majewski* rule, notwithstanding the sanguine view we express above.[146]

THE RELEVANCE OF VOLUNTARY INTOXICATION TO ATTEMPT AND CONSPIRACY

2.106 In the previous paragraphs we introduced the problem which may arise as a result of the use of the term "reckless" in Part 2 of the Serious Crime Act 2007.

2.107 Recklessness as to a circumstance element already suffices for the purposes of the inchoate offence of attempt, contrary to section 1 of the Criminal Attempts Act 1981, even though subsection (1) requires proof that D "intended" to commit the relevant substantive offence.[147]

2.108 For D to be convicted of attempting to commit offence X, D must have intended his or her act and intended the consequence (if any) required for a person to be liable for offence X. However, if the definition of offence X has a circumstance element and a fault requirement that D acted recklessly with regard to it, then, if D is charged with attempting to commit offence X, D need only have been reckless with regard to that circumstance element. It is not necessary for the prosecution to prove that D "intended" the circumstance element to be present (or that D knew or believed the circumstance element existed or would exist).[148]

2.109 The question whether the *Majewski* rule applies to recklessness as to a circumstance element, in a case where D is charged with attempt under the 1981 Act, has not yet been considered by the Court of Appeal. Nevertheless, should the matter arise for consideration it is likely that the *Majewski* rule would be applied in the same way that it has been applied to the fault element for the completed offence.

---

[146] Paragraphs 2.100 to 2.101.

[147] Section 1(1) provides as follows: "If, with intent to commit an offence to which [section 1] applies, a person does an act which is more than merely preparatory to the commission of the offence, he is guilty of attempting to commit the offence."

[148] See Law Com Consultation Paper No 183 (2007), Conspiracy and Attempts, para 14.39. As we argue in the CP, it is an important principle of inchoate offences that they should require at least recklessness as to a circumstance element to be proved, unless the substantive offence requires proof of a more stringent fault element.

2.110   Our reason for saying this is that there is very little difference between the moral culpability of the person who successfully commits an offence requiring recklessness as to a circumstance element, and a person who tries but fails to commit that offence. It is often merely a matter of chance whether D succeeds or fails in his or her attempt to commit an offence, and D can be liable for attempt only if he or she goes beyond the stage of mere preparation. It would make little sense to have one rule on voluntary intoxication for the case where D is charged with having committed offence X, and a separate rule for the case where D is charged with having attempted to commit offence X. Different rules would make the law especially difficult for a tribunal of fact to understand and apply when D is charged with both the substantive and the inchoate offence. (For example, D may be charged with murder and attempted murder in the alternative, on the ground that it may not be possible to prove that D's act caused V's death.)

2.111   At present it is not possible to convict D of conspiracy on the basis of recklessness as to a circumstance element, even where such recklessness is sufficient for the agreed substantive offence. The issue regarding the application of the *Majewski* rule is therefore currently of no relevance in this context.

PART 3
INTOXICATION AND FAULT – RECOMMENDATIONS

THE COMMISSION'S PREVIOUS RECOMMENDATIONS

3.1 As explained in Part 1,[1] the Law Commission undertook a review of the law on intoxication prior to publishing its 1992 Consultation Paper No 127, Intoxication and Criminal Liability, and its final recommendations in Legislating the Criminal Code: Intoxication and Criminal Liability (1995), Law Com No 229 ("the 1995 report"). The recommendations in the 1995 report were designed to supersede the intoxication provisions in the Draft Criminal Law Bill appended to Law Com No 218[2] and the relevant provisions in the original Draft Criminal Code Bill.[3]

Law Commission Consultation Paper No 127 – radical reform

3.2 The Commission originally objected to the *Majewski* rule[4] for three principal reasons:[5]

(1) there is an absence of satisfactory criteria for determining whether a crime is one of "basic intent" or one of "specific intent";

(2) the piecemeal approach to the development of the law has led to the underlying policy being implemented in an erratic and unprincipled way;

(3) it is unclear whether self-induced intoxication is to be regarded as equivalent to the mental state required by the definition of the offence for liability, or whether the jury are supposed to consider the hypothetical question whether D *would* have had that mental state had he or she been sober.[6]

3.3 The Commission's view was that the *Majewski* rule should be abolished, so that D's intoxication would be taken into account when determining whether he or she had the state of mind required for liability by the definition of the offence charged. A further proposal was that there should be a new offence of criminal intoxication, for which D would be liable if he or she caused harm while "deliberately intoxicated to a substantial extent".

---

[1] Paragraphs 1.63 to 1.66.

[2] Offences Against the Person and General Principles (1993) Law Com No 218. See Law Com No 229, para 1.13.

[3] A Criminal Code for England and Wales: Report and Draft Criminal Code Bill (1989), Law Com No 177. Appendix B, below, sets out earlier recommendations made by the Commission and other bodies.

[4] Paragraph 2.37 above.

[5] Legislating the Criminal Code: Intoxication and Criminal Liability (1995), Law Com No 229, p 42. See generally Consultation Paper No 127, Part III.

[6] This problem may have been overstated. The latter alternative must surely be correct as a matter of common sense, given the various possible degrees of "intoxication" and that there may be a number of alternative reasons for not foreseeing a particular eventuality.

3.4 The provisional proposal in 1993 was a version of the approach originally suggested by the Butler Committee in 1975 and subsequently reformulated with improvements by Professors John Smith and Glanville Williams for consideration by the Criminal Law Revision Committee in 1980.[7] This was not, however, the approach eventually recommended in the 1995 report.

Law Com No 229 – a return to codification

3.5 The Commission gave a number of reasons for discarding its provisional proposals, in favour of codification of the common law, in paragraphs 1.26 to 1.33 of the 1995 report.

3.6 First, following consultation, it became apparent that there was little if any support for the abolition of the *Majewski* rule or the creation of a new offence of criminal intoxication. With regard to the proposed new offence:

> there was an almost unanimous rejection of [it] by practitioner bodies. There was an additional category of respondents who supported the new offence subject to a range of qualifications that, in our view, would have largely defeated its purpose.[8]

3.7 Respondents gave the following reasons for rejecting (or qualifying) this proposal:[9]

(1) the real likelihood that the offence of criminal intoxication would be regarded as a less serious offence, and would result in more trials and/or the raising of more issues at trial than is currently the case;

(2) the likelihood of expert evidence being called on the question whether or not D's awareness or control was "substantially impaired" would result in even lengthier trials;

(3) the police would have to devote more time to enquiries into the extent of D's intake of intoxicants prior to the commission of the alleged offence;

(4) there could be practical difficulties for the prosecution with regard to whether, or when, an alternative count (that is, criminal intoxication) should be added to the indictment;[10]

(5) the offence would need to incorporate an element of causation to prevent D being liable for a genuine accident which unluckily occurred while he or she was intoxicated, and which might have occurred even if D had been sober.

---

[7] Fourteenth Report, *Offences Against the Person*, (1980) Cmnd 7844, pp 113 to 114. See Appendix B below.

[8] Legislating the Criminal Code: Intoxication and Criminal Liability (1995), Law Com No 229, para 1.26.

[9] Above, pp 43 to 44. Unsurprisingly, some of the criticisms overlap with those raised by the CLRC against a similar proposal put forward by Professors Smith and Williams.

[10] This objection is weaker now that D is under a pre-trial obligation to disclose his or her defence.

3.8   Secondly, in the absence of any acceptable replacement for the *Majewski* rule, the Commission felt unable to support a proposal that the rule be abolished even though there was some support for this approach.[11] The Commission accepted the view of the judges of the Queen's Bench Division that an acquittal on the ground of self-induced intoxication, and the absence of a conviction for a lesser (alternative) offence reflecting the same conduct, "would be perceived by the public as unacceptable . . . with the result that damage would be done to public confidence in the judicial system".[12] The Commission noted, moreover, that abolition of the *Majewski* rule without replacement could also lead to intoxication from uncommon drugs being raised as a defence in many trials, and that it might be difficult for the prosecution to disprove defences of this sort to the criminal standard.[13]

3.9   The third reason for abandoning the proposed abolition of the *Majewski* rule was that, in the view of the respondents to the Commission's Consultation Paper No 127, tribunals of fact did not in practice experience as much difficulty with the common law approach as the Commission had originally assumed:

> the judiciary (including the majority of the Queen's Bench judges), the Law Society and many others found that the *Majewski* doctrine worked fairly and without any undue difficulty. We found the overall weight of these arguments convincing ...[14]

3.10   This left two alternatives: either do nothing, or codify the law in a way which would clarify the *Majewski* rule and resolve the problems associated with it.[15] The Commission chose the latter option:

> The results of consultation had persuaded us that the *Majewski* approach operated fairly, on the whole, and without undue difficulty, but that it was both desirable and necessary to set out the relevant principles clearly in codified form.[16]

---

[11]   The Criminal Bar Association Working Party supported abolition because there were so few cases in practice where D was so intoxicated that he or she did not have the state of mind for liability. Professor Sir John Smith approved abolition "in principle", but recognised the possibility of public outrage should a violent drunk not be convicted of any offence after he or she had caused serious injury.

[12]   Legislating the Criminal Code: Intoxication and Criminal Liability (1995), Law Com No 229, paras 1.27 and 5.22.

[13]   Above, para 5.27.

[14]   Above, para 1.28. See also para 5.29.

[15]   The other options – to disregard the effect of voluntary intoxication in all cases, even where the alleged offence was one of "specific intent"; and to disregard the effect of voluntary intoxication in all cases, subject to a reverse onus defence which would allow D to prove absence of fault – were regarded as unacceptable in both Consultation Paper 127 and Law Com No 229. There was no significant evidence of support for either option following consultation.

[16]   Legislating the Criminal Code: Intoxication and Criminal Liability (1995), Law Com No 229, para 1.32.

3.11   We accept, in broad terms, that this is the right approach. The principal aspects of the present common law on intoxication and criminal liability should be set out in legislation.

3.12   We appreciate that this approach may be regarded by purists as contrary to legal principle, because D may be convicted of an offence even though he or she did not have the state of mind required for liability by its definition. Our view, however, is that this objection to the *Majewski* rule is based on an unduly narrow view of criminal liability which pays insufficient regard to the legitimacy of any exception to the general position.[17]

3.13   In the present context, where we are primarily concerned with the conviction and punishment of aggressive individuals who cause damage or bodily harm following self-induced intoxication, we agree with Stephen Gough's view that "absolute subjectivism is an unattractive and unnatural standpoint".[18]

Law Com No 229 – the Draft Criminal Law (Intoxication) Bill

3.14   The Commission's (1995) Draft Criminal Law (Intoxication) Bill ("the 1995 Bill") appended to the 1995 report[19] consists of eight clauses. Nevertheless the Home Office took the view that it was too complex:[20]

> Since [the publication in 1993 of Law Com No 218][21] the Law Commission has made separate recommendations about replacing the *Majewski* rules in statute law in their report "Intoxication in the Criminal Law" (LC 122) [*sic*].[22] The Government considered these proposals, but thought that they were unnecessarily complex for the purposes of this [Offences Against the Person] Bill.

3.15   The complexity of the 1995 Bill also attracted criticism from other quarters:[23]

---

[17]   See paras 1.49 to 1.55 above.

[18]   S Gough, "Intoxication and Criminal Liability: The Law Commission's Proposed Reforms" (1996) 112 *Law Quarterly Review* 335, 337.

[19]   Legislating the Criminal Code: Intoxication and Criminal Liability (1995), Law Com No 229.

[20]   *Violence, Reforming the Offences Against the Person Act 1861* (1998), para 3.23.

[21]   Offences Against the Person and General Principles (1993). See paras B.11 to B.16 below (Appendix B).

[22]   The Home Office meant Legislating the Criminal Code: Intoxication and Criminal Liability (1995), Law Com No 229.

[23]   In contrast, J O'Leary focused his criticism on the Commission's volte-face: O'Leary, "Lament for the Intoxication 'Defence'" (1997) 48 *Northern Ireland Law Quarterly* 152.

> [The Commission's] proposals are geared to dealing with intoxication that renders conduct inadvertent and a complex set of additional rules are introduced to deal with intoxication resulting in mistake or automatism. Apart from its untidiness, this unnecessary complexity encourages legalistic argument and conceals dangerous loopholes and inconsistencies. ... the Commission seems to be overthinking its argument, to be founding unnecessary distinctions on irrelevant differences.[24]

> [T]he report conducts [a] disproportionately detailed analysis of some relatively unlikely situations, culminating in clauses 5 and 6 of the Bill, which contain a total of 24 sub-clauses. ... [T]he abominable clause 6 and its nine sub-clauses ... deal solely with the case of someone who consumes one intoxicant unaware it has been laced with another intoxicant. ... It is difficult to see how this provision contributes to the "greater clarity and accessibility" ... codification is intended to bring, and hard to resist the conclusion that some eventualities are better left to judicial interpretation. ... Ironically, the most likely legislative outcome ... may be a return to the intoxication provisions of the Offences Against the Person Report. These implement the preferred policy with considerably more economy and clarity than do some of the new report's tortured provisions.[25]

3.16 We accept that the 1995 Bill is to some extent complex, perhaps unnecessarily so in places, although it should be noted that in some important respects it is insufficiently comprehensive (for example, secondary liability was not addressed). We acknowledge, in particular, that some concepts are best left undefined, to allow for the development of the law as novel circumstances arise, and that criminal legislation should not seek to lay down a detailed set of rules with a view to addressing every conceivable set of facts. This is why we say in paragraph 3.11, above, that the principal aspects of the present common law on intoxication and criminal liability should be set out in legislation; and why we believe that the common law governing this area should not be expressly abolished.[26]

3.17 The approach we have decided to adopt, therefore, is to build upon the central recommendations in the 1995 report but give effect to them in a new draft Bill which covers the key areas of the law in a less elaborate way. We set out our recommendations below. Our new draft Criminal Law (Intoxication) Bill is set out with explanatory notes in Appendix A.

---

[24] S Gough, "Intoxication and Criminal Liability: The Law Commission's Proposed Reforms" (1996) 112 *Law Quarterly Review* 335, 339 and 351. Gough also criticises the Commission's approach to causation, and the proposed abolition of the courts' ability to decide on a case-by-case basis which offences should be offences of "basic intent" and which should be offences of "specific intent".

[25] E Paton, "Reformulating the Intoxication Rules: The Law Commission's Report" [1995] *Criminal Law Review* 382, 386 to 387 and 388.

[26] See para 3.26 below.

RECOMMENDATIONS (1) – VOLUNTARY INTOXICATION

Introduction

3.18 Our underlying approach for self-induced intoxication is to maintain the present common law position between two equally unattractive extremes.[27] We intend to provide a clearer exposition of the law to ensure that it is easier to understand and therefore easier to apply in practice.

3.19 A related aspect of our recommendations is to ensure that the law is understood both in its application to alleged perpetrators and also in relation to any person who is alleged to have encouraged or assisted a perpetrator. In other words, the law should be clear for the situation where the accused is alleged to have perpetrated the offence charged, and equally clear for the situation where D is an alleged accessory.

3.20 In a similar vein, we also recommend a clear, comprehensive and internally-consistent approach for the situation where D wishes to rely on a defence based on his or her mistaken understanding of the circumstances, where the mistake resulted from voluntary intoxication.[28]

3.21 We take the view, therefore, that legislation should be enacted which would expressly list the types of subjective fault element which should always be proved by the prosecution.

3.22 This statutory list should include:

(1) the states of mind which have been held to be "specific intents" at common law;

(2) the states of mind which would no doubt be regarded as "specific intents" at common law should the issue arise; and

(3) the states of mind which should in any event be treated as "specific intents" as a matter of principle, on the ground that the commission of the external element of the offence with the required state of mind is fundamentally different from the commission of the external element without that state of mind through voluntary intoxication.[29]

3.23 The legislation to which we refer should exclude the concept of subjective recklessness from this list of fault elements. Our recommendation, in line with the Commission's previous recommendation and the position at common law, is that subjective recklessness should not need to be proved if D's lack of awareness was caused by voluntary intoxication.[30]

---

[27] See paras 1.48 to 1.62 above.

[28] Specific statutory defences relating to D's state of mind are to be treated as aspects of the fault element rather than "defences" if the courts have held that the defence is in effect a denial of fault and that it is for the prosecution to prove the relevant culpable state of mind. See para 3.79 below and cl 1(2) of our new Criminal Law (Intoxication) Bill.

[29] See para 2.14 above.

[30] This is subject to one narrow exception, explained in paras 3.104 to 3.117 below.

3.24   We believe the legislation should also:

(1)   set out a clear, definitive test to be applied in cases where subjective recklessness is alleged and D was voluntarily intoxicated;

(2)   provide a single rule for any situation where D wishes to rely on a general defence to which his or her state of mind is relevant, if D's state of mind was affected by voluntary intoxication;

(3)   provide a body of rules which would allow the court to determine, without difficulty, whether or not D was voluntarily intoxicated at the relevant time; and

(4)   expressly provide for the situation where it is alleged that D encouraged or assisted a perpetrator (P) to commit an offence and is liable for the offence on that basis (as an "accessory").

3.25   Nevertheless, as explained above,[31] we believe it would be wholly inappropriate to try to legislate at the microscopic level, whereby each and every conceivable factual scenario involving voluntary intoxication is expressly addressed. We also take the view that, as ordinary English terms which would be readily understood by the courts, "intoxicant" and "voluntary intoxication" do not need to be defined in legislation.

3.26   We therefore reject the over-inclusiveness of the 1995 Bill[32] in favour of a more open-textured approach which, if adopted, would retain certain aspects of the common law. Our new draft Bill does not expressly abolish the common law rules on intoxication. For unusual situations not covered by the legislation the common law would survive and evolve to fill any lacunae as they are identified.[33]

3.27   In particular, our new draft Bill does not contain provisions which would address the following situations:

(1)   D acts in a state of automatism caused by a combination of voluntary intoxication and the impact of an external agent such as a blow to the head.

(2)   D commits the external element of an offence under the combined effects of voluntary intoxication and a mental abnormality.

---

[31]   Paragraph 3.16.

[32]   See clauses 5 and 6 of the 1995 Bill.

[33]   The common law rules would be impliedly abolished to the extent that the legislation addresses the same area, but not otherwise.

3.28 Of course, if D is disadvantaged by a mental abnormality, and that abnormality was entirely (or almost entirely) the reason for his or her mistake or unawareness, D should be able to rely on insanity as a defence even if D was also affected by an intoxicant at the relevant time. Equally, if D's mistake or unawareness was entirely or almost entirely caused by the effects of an external agent, regardless of any effect attributable to intoxication, then D should be able to rely on the defence of automatism.

3.29 Conversely, if the effects of the mental abnormality or external agent were insignificant when compared with the effects of the voluntarily-consumed intoxicant, then it is right that D's liability should be resolved by the application of our recommended rules on voluntary intoxication.

3.30 In our view, however, we would not be serving any useful purpose if we were expressly to provide as much in our new draft Bill or, more to the point, if we were to try to cater in our draft Bill for the various possibilities between the extremes to which we refer.[34]

3.31 We believe the law governing unusual situations of this sort should be left to the courts, to be developed incrementally as cases arise.

Specific recommendations

3.32 In the following paragraphs we set out our specific recommendations for the law on criminal liability and voluntary intoxication. In each case we set out our recommendation first (in **bold** type). We then provide an explanation for the recommendation and a reference to the relevant provision in our new draft Criminal Liability (Intoxication) Bill.[35]

3.33 The common law terms "basic intent" and "specific intent" are not used in our draft Bill. As explained above, however, we do retain the common law approach whereby:

(1) some subjective fault elements must always be proved (in which case D's state of voluntary intoxication is relevant to the determination of D's liability); and

(2) some subjective fault elements, subjective recklessness in particular, do not always need to be proved (in which case D's state of voluntary intoxication is irrelevant to the determination of D's liability).

---

[34] The only justification for being wholly conclusive on this issue would be to ensure that D would not receive an absolute acquittal if he or she was affected by self-induced intoxication and a mental abnormality of a type which would be likely to cause D to act in the same way again (see *Burns* (1973) 58 Cr App R 364). However, the Court of Appeal's suggestion in that case (para 2.93 above) is best regarded as an aberration, and we doubt whether it would be followed.

[35] The Bill is set out in full in Appendix A.

3.34   We do not wish to cause confusion by retaining the term "specific intent" in this Part as a label for states of mind falling within the category of fault elements described by paragraph 3.33(1). Our new draft Bill is silent on what such states of mind should be called. We have therefore opted to use the label "integral fault element" in the following paragraphs to describe any such state of mind. The intention to kill or cause grievous bodily harm, the fault element for murder, is an integral fault element because it has a constitutive role to play in defining murder as a wrong. It is not simply an element of culpability attached to a wrong defined by the external elements of the offence.

Recommendation 1: the Majewski rule

3.35   There should be a general rule that:

> **(1)   if D is charged with having committed an offence as a perpetrator;**
>
> **(2)   the fault element of the offence is not an integral fault element (for example, because it merely requires proof of recklessness);[36] and**
>
> **(3)   D was voluntarily intoxicated at the material time;**
>
> **then, in determining whether or not D is liable for the offence, D should be treated as having been aware at the material time of anything which D would then have been aware of but for the intoxication.[37]**

3.36   The approach we recommend would apply regardless of the degree to which D was intoxicated and regardless of whether D's state of intoxication was caused by alcohol or some other drug or substance (such as a solvent) or any combination of intoxicants.

3.37   We include recklessness within the scope of this general rule as an "example", but the practical effect of the rule, when read with the exceptions,[38] would be to limit the application of the rule to allegations of recklessness.[39] The effects of self-induced intoxication would be disregarded whether the offence charged requires proof of subjective recklessness[40] or objective ("Caldwell") recklessness.[41]

3.38   If the allegation is one of subjective recklessness, D would be treated as having been aware of any risk or circumstance D *would* have been aware of but for his or her self-induced state of intoxication.

---

[36]   This is subject to one narrow exception, explained in paras 3.104 to 3.117 below.

[37]   New Criminal Law (Intoxication) Bill, cl 3(1) to (3). The integral fault elements not covered by the general rule are listed in cl 3(5). The position for insanity (and automatism) would continue to be governed by the common law; see paras 3.27 to 3.31 above and cl 9(4) of the new Criminal Law (Intoxication) Bill.

[38]   Paragraphs 3.46 and 3.104 below.

[39]   It is possible, but not likely, that the subjective fault requirement of an offence may be defined in terms of "likelihood" or "foresight of a probability". If so, any such state of mind would also be covered by the general rule on the ground that it does not fall within the exhaustive list of integral fault elements (cl 3(5)).

[40]   Paragraph 1.12(4) above

[41]   Paragraph 1.12(7) above.

3.39   If the allegation is one of *Caldwell* objective recklessness,[42] D would be regarded as reckless because of the objective nature of the test and the irrelevance of the intoxication when applying it.[43] And if D were to argue that he or she was not "*Caldwell* reckless" because D had considered the question of risk and mistakenly concluded (as a result of self-induced intoxication) that there was no risk, or that the risk was so small that it would be reasonable to take it, D would be liable if D *would* have been aware of the true nature of the risk if he or she had not been voluntarily intoxicated.[44]

3.40   Our recommendation follows the approach recommended by the Commission in the 1995 report:

>   the best way of codifying the present law, whilst avoiding the problems inherent in the present distinction between offences of specific and of basic intent, is to confine the *Majewski* principle, broadly speaking, to offences for which proof of recklessness (or awareness of risk) is sufficient. ... it has the advantages of simplicity and clarity, both matters of great importance in any system of criminal law.[45]

>   the jury would be directed to disregard [D's] lack of awareness *only* to the extent that it was caused by the intoxication rather than [for example] illness. This approach has the merit of ensuring that [D] would not be penalised in so far as his condition was caused by matters other than the intoxication.[46] ... we were persuaded by our consultation that, so far as can be known, juries have no difficulty with this hypothetical question.[47] Furthermore ... [it] is the question that in principle the jury *ought* to address.[48]

---

[42]   Insofar as the test has survived the decision of the House of Lords in *G* [2003] UKHL 50, [2004] 1 AC 1034 (see fn 27 in Part 1, above).

[43]   Where the definition of a fault element refers to, or requires reference to, the state of mind or conduct to be expected of a reasonable person, such person is one who is not intoxicated to any extent. Our new draft Criminal Law (Intoxication) Bill does not provide for this situation because it is unnecessary to do so. The Bill provides rules for the situation where D's liability requires proof of a "fault element which depends upon D's state of mind" (cl 1(1)(b)). The position for no-fault offences and negligence, and for *Caldwell* recklessness where D's state of mind is irrelevant, continues to be covered by the common law.

[44]   This aspect of *Caldwell* recklessness *is* covered by the general rule in cl 3((3) of our new draft Criminal Law (Intoxication) Bill because D's liability requires proof of a "fault element which depends upon D's state of mind" (cl 1(1)(b)).

[45]   Legislating the Criminal Code: Intoxication and Criminal Liability (1995), Law Com No 229, paras 6.6 to 6.7.

[46]   Above, para 6.29 (emphasis in original).

[47]   Above, para 6.32.

[48]   Above, para 6.33 (emphasis in original).

3.41   If an offence may be committed intentionally or recklessly, such as the offence of common assault, the prosecution might wish to formulate the particulars of the charge in the alternative forms should the factual nature of the allegation warrant such an approach. If the *intent* (an integral fault element)[49] for the more serious allegation could not be proved, D would nevertheless be liable for the *reckless* form of the offence. Of course if it would not be possible to prove the required intent, because of the extent of D's self-induced intoxication, the prosecution would be free to allege only the reckless form of the offence.

Recommendation 2: the rule for integral fault elements

3.42   **If the subjective fault element in the definition of the offence, as alleged, is one to which the justification for the *Majewski* rule does not apply, then the prosecution should have to prove that D acted with that relevant state of mind.**

3.43   In paragraph 3.22 above we set out the basis for determining which fault elements should be excluded from the application of the general (*Majewski*) rule. For such fault elements, evidence of D's voluntary intoxication should be taken into consideration by the court when determining whether the prosecution has proved that D acted (or failed to act) with the required state of mind. We list the integral fault elements below under our next recommendation.

3.44   Importantly, it would be *the particular state of mind* alleged by the prosecution, not the offence itself, which would determine whether the general rule applies. Our recommendation would abandon the courts' unhelpful categorisation which distinguishes between *offences* of "specific intent" and *offences* of "basic intent".[50] This accords with the Commission's policy in the 1995 report.[51]

3.45   If recklessness is alleged then, as explained above, the general rule would apply. But if the prosecution alleges that D acted with an integral fault element, it would be necessary to prove that D had that required state of mind at the relevant time; and the jury would be directed that D's intoxication should be taken into account in determining whether the allegation has been proved.

Recommendation 3: the integral fault elements

3.46   **The following subjective fault elements should be excluded from the application of the general rule and should, therefore, always be proved:[52]**

---

49   Paragraph 3.46 below.

50   See paras 2.2 to 2.10 above. See also White, "Offences of Basic and Specific Intent" [1989] *Criminal Law Review* 271, 272:

> since proof of intent will always suffice for offences that can be committed recklessly, we cannot say that such offences are (always) ones of basic intent. What any such offence actually is in any particular instance will depend upon which type of [fault element] the prosecution seeks to prove.

51   Legislating the Criminal Code: Intoxication and Criminal Liability (1995), Law Com No 229, para 6.8.

52   New Criminal Law (Intoxication) Bill, cl 3(4) to (6).

(1) intention as to a consequence;[53]

(2) knowledge as to something;[54]

(3) belief as to something (where the belief is equivalent to knowledge as to something);[55]

(4) fraud; and

(5) dishonesty.

3.47 Two other states of mind we recommend for inclusion within this category of subjective fault elements are explained below, in their proper context, under the heading "Specific recommendations for those who assist or encourage crime".[56]

3.48 The list of integral fault elements we recommend would be exhaustive. The question in all cases would be whether the state of mind required by the definition of the offence does or does not fall within the list. Recklessness, as a general concept, is excluded from our list of integral fault elements, so, as explained above, if the prosecution alleges recklessness the general (*Majewski*) rule would apply.

3.49 However, the courts would continue to have a degree of latitude as to the applicability or non-applicability of the general rule, to the extent that where the definition of an offence, as alleged, has an *implicit* requirement of subjective fault which has not previously been addressed:

(1) it would be for the courts to decide, as a preliminary issue, what exactly that state of mind is; and

(2) in reaching its decision as to the nature of the state of mind, the courts would be aware of the different rules which apply in cases of voluntary intoxication and the arguments which support or militate against the application of the general rule.

3.50 For example, where the fault element of an offence is defined with the word "allow" or "permit", the courts could interpret the provision to include, implicitly, nothing more than an awareness of a possibility (a form of subjective recklessness encompassed by the general rule) or to include an implicit requirement of knowledge (an integral fault element).

3.51 A relevant consideration when determining the nature of the fault element would no doubt be whether, assuming the implicit fault element is an integral fault element, there is an alternative offence of recklessness for which D could be held liable.

[53] But not intention as to conduct.

[54] But not knowledge as to a risk, which falls within the scope of subjective recklessness.

[55] This is a belief amounting to a certainty or near-certainty that something was, is or will be the case (drawing in part on the concept of indirect intention explained in para 1.12(1) and fn 19 in Part 1 above).

[56] Paragraphs 3.88 to 3.117.

3.52   Section 1 of the Dangerous Dogs Act 1991[57] provides an example of the type of offence we have in mind. The courts would have to decide, and make an explicit ruling on, the question whether the implicit concept of awareness, where D has "allowed" an unmuzzled dangerous dog to be in a public place, should be held to require proof of knowledge or belief (integral fault elements) or proof of a broader state of mind encompassed by the general rule for intoxication and liability.[58]

Recommendation 4 (defences and mistaken beliefs)

3.53   **D should not be able to rely on a mistake of fact arising from self-induced intoxication in support of a defence to which D's state of mind is relevant, regardless of the nature of the fault alleged. D's mistaken belief should be taken into account only if D would have held the same belief if D had not been intoxicated.[59]**

3.54   In this respect we depart from a recommendation previously made by the Commission. That recommendation was that the common law rule requiring proof of "specific intents" (integral fault elements) should be extended to apply to defences relied on by D if D is charged with an offence of "specific intent". So, for example, if D wished to rely on a mistake in support of the defence of self-defence, in response to an allegation of murder, D would be permitted to rely on any mistake as to the circumstances, even a mistake caused by voluntary intoxication.[60]

3.55   There are several reasons why we now recommend an alternative approach which accords with the present law.[61] However, it may be helpful if we first explain, with reference to murder and self-defence, why the present legal position has been criticised.[62]

3.56   As the law stands, in a case of alleged murder D can rely on evidence of his self-induced intoxication to show that he or she did not act with the intent to kill or to cause grievous bodily harm to another person. By way of contrast, D cannot rely on such evidence to show that he or she was mistaken as to the factual circumstances relevant to the claim that D believed he or she faced an attack by the deceased. It follows that D who

---

[57]   Paragraph 2.12 above.

[58]   We accept that the courts would probably adopt the latter interpretation, given the judgment in *DPP v Kellet* (1994) 158 JP 1138, para 2.12 above.

[59]   New Criminal Law (Intoxication) Bill, cl 5(3)(b). However, the position for insanity (and automatism) would continue to be governed by the common law; see paras 3.27 to 3.31 above and cl 9(4) of the new Criminal Law (Intoxication) Bill.

[60]   A Criminal Code for England and Wales: Report and Draft Criminal Code Bill (1989), Vol 2, para 8.42; Legislating the Criminal Code: Intoxication and Criminal Liability (1995), Law Com No 229, paras 7.9 to 7.12.

[61]   For the present law on this area, see paras 2.47 to 2.62 above.

[62]   Criticisms in the academic literature can be found in: H Milgate [1987] *Cambridge Law Journal* 381; JC Smith [1987] *Criminal Law Review* 706; F McAuley, "The Intoxication Defence in Criminal Law" (1997) 32 *Irish Jurist* 243; *Smith and Hogan, Criminal Law* (12th ed, 2008) at p 308; and JR Spencer, "Drunken Defence" [2006] *Cambridge Law Journal* 267.

by reason of intoxication, kills his victim in the mistaken belief that he is acting in self-defence has no defence; but [D] is entitled to an acquittal [in respect of murder] if the effect of his mistake ... induces him to believe he is killing ... an orangutang.[63]

3.57 There is no liability for murder if D's intention is to kill something other than a human being, such as an ape. This is because it is permissible for D to rely on a mistake induced by voluntary intoxication insofar as it relates to the presence or absence of the intent to kill or cause grievous bodily harm to a person.

3.58 The critics' argument is one of consistency. If D is charged with having committed murder, D can rely on voluntary intoxication to rebut the allegation that he or she acted with the culpable state of mind required for liability. So, it should equally be permissible for D to rely on a factual mistake caused by voluntary intoxication if the mistake relates to a surrounding circumstance affecting D's perception of whether reasonable force in self-defence was required.[64] This is the argument we reject.

3.59 Our first reason for rejecting the critics' argument is that it fails to address the important fact that self-defence is a *general* defence and that, accordingly, it is a defence which should in principle be available on the same basis in relation to all crimes, regardless of the nature of the fault alleged. The law should give the same answer as to its availability whatever the crime may be, whether it be an offence requiring proof of an integral fault element or an offence defined with a fault element of recklessness. The law should not draw an anomalous distinction between cases which require proof of an integral fault element and cases where mere recklessness is alleged, given that D's belief – as to the need to take certain supposedly necessary defensive steps – is identical in all cases, regardless of the nature of the allegation.

---

[63] F McAuley, "The Intoxication Defence in Criminal Law" (1997) 32 *Irish Jurist* 243, 265. A similar example was used in B Fisse (ed), *Howard's Criminal Law* (5th ed, 1990) at pp 514 to 515:

> Assume that D takes self-defensive action on the strength of an honest yet unreasonable belief that he is under vicious attack by V1, a person dressed in a gorilla suit but whom D believes to be a psychotic human assailant; V1 is killed. If D's belief as to the situation confronting him must be reasonable he cannot successfully plead self-defence and will be liable for murder. Assume the same case except that D believes that he is under vicious attack by V2, a person also dressed in a gorilla suit but whom he believes to be a psychotic gorilla; V2 is killed. Although the belief is also unreasonable D is not liable for murder because he does not realise that he is using lethal force against a human being. In terms of culpability there seems to be no material distinction between these two situations.

[64] See JR Spencer, "Drunken Defence" [2006] *Cambridge Law Journal* 267, 268: "If Hamlet, high on drugs, kills Polonius because he honestly but unreasonably believes the shape behind the arras is a rat, he has the benefit of his mistake and his crime is manslaughter at most ... But if he does the same thing in the equally honest but unreasonable belief that Polonius is an assassin lurking there to kill him, his crime ... is murder."

3.60   The present law in this respect, which we recommend should be retained, does give a single answer. The Court of Appeal has on three occasions said that self-defence is not available, whatever the crime charged, if the mistake D made as to the circumstances was caused by voluntary intoxication.[65] In *O'Grady*,[66] regarded as binding in *Hatton*,[67] Lord Lane CJ said the following:

> where the jury are satisfied that the defendant was mistaken in his belief that any force or the force which he in fact used was necessary to defend himself and are further satisfied that the mistake was caused by voluntarily induced intoxication, the defence [of self-defence] must fail. We do not consider that any distinction should be drawn on this aspect of the matter between offences involving what is called specific intent, such as murder, and offences of so-called basic intent, such as manslaughter. Quite apart from the problem of directing a jury in a case such as the present where manslaughter is an alternative verdict to murder, the question of mistake can and ought to be considered separately from the question of intent.[68]

3.61   Lord Lane did not explain why "the question of mistake can and ought to be considered separately from the question of intent", but one can readily discern an important distinction between

(1)   the situation where D1 intentionally kills another person (V1) in the mistaken belief that V1 is about to attack D1, where D1's mistake is caused solely by his or her being drunk; and

(2)   the situation where D2 avoids liability for murder on the ground that he or she drunkenly mistook a person (V2) for an ape, and killed V2 for that reason.

---

[65]   *O'Grady* [1987] QB 995, *O'Connor* [1991] *Criminal Law Review* 135, *Hatton* [2005] EWCA Crim 2951, [2006] 1 Cr App R 16 (247).

[66]   [1987] QB 995.

[67]   [2005] EWCA Crim 2951, [2006] 1 Cr App R 16 (247).

[68]   [1987] QB 995, 999.

3.62 The difference is that, in the first situation, D is aware that he or she is inflicting harm against a *person* and therefore that his or her conduct requires a truly compelling justification or excuse. As Professor Simester argues, D "is asserting a liberty, based upon circumstances, to inflict harm *knowingly*" and, accordingly, "it does not seem too much to ask for reasonable ascertainment of such circumstances".[69] D should not therefore be permitted to rely on an unreasonable mistake caused by voluntary intoxication when D knowingly inflicts harm on another person. By contrast, in the second situation D believes, albeit unreasonably, that he or she is killing an ape.[70]

3.63 Our second reason for rejecting the critics' argument relates to what Lord Lane said about directing the jury in cases where D is charged with murder. Allowing a distinction to be drawn between the situation where the prosecution alleges an integral fault element and the situation where no such element is alleged would be difficult to apply and extremely confusing for the jury. If the jury were to be directed to take into account D's intoxicated state when considering a mistake in relation to murder, but not manslaughter, where self-defence is relied on, it would also be necessary to direct the jury to determine whether, given that mistake, the degree of force used by D was reasonable.[71] In this respect D's intoxicated state would be disregarded, for the test is objective, but it is difficult to see how any jury would be able to make much sense of the idea of an objectively proportionate response to a mistaken threat which is wholly unreasonable on account of being induced by a state of intoxication. For example, if, through taking drugs, D kills V in the intoxicated belief that they were in a video game, and D thought that V was about to cast a fatal spell on him, and that he therefore had to act in self-defence, could we sensibly expect a jury to determine an objectively appropriate reaction?[72]

---

[69] AP Simester, 'Mistakes in Defence' (1992) 12 *Oxford Journal of Legal Studies* 295, 309 (emphasis in original).

[70] We accept, however, that the courts have concluded that a successful claim to self-defence means that D did not act with the fault required for liability, because the intention to kill or cause grievous bodily harm carries an additional implicit requirement of unlawfulness. That is to say, *technically*, the fault for murder is the intention to kill or cause serious harm unlawfully (see *Williams (Gladstone)* (1983) 78 Cr App R 276 and *Beckford* [1988] AC 130). But compare AP Simester, 'Mistakes in Defence' (1992) 12 *Oxford Journal of Legal Studies* 295. The thrust of Professor Simester's article is that *Williams (Gladstone)* was wrongly decided in this respect because, in his view, by raising self-defence D is not asserting that a constituent element of the offence is lacking. Rather, D is raising a defence in relation to conduct which on the face of it constitutes an offence.

[71] Criminal Justice and Immigration Act 2008, s 76(3).

[72] A further complication has been introduced by s 76(7)(b) of the Criminal Justice and Immigration Act 2008, which may require the jury to be told, in deciding whether the degree of force used by D was reasonable, that "evidence of a person's having only done what the person honestly and instinctively thought was necessary for a legitimate purpose constitutes strong evidence that only reasonable action was taken by that person for that purpose".

3.64   Our third reason for agreeing with the current legal position is that Parliament has very recently considered this aspect of the law and concluded that it should not be permissible for D to avoid liability for murder, based on self-defence, if D's claim is based on a mistake induced by voluntary intoxication. It is the Government's policy that the law should remain as it is in this respect, and Parliament has agreed.[73]

3.65   There would need to be a very sound argument for changing the law to justify our reaching a different view from that of Parliament, in relation to legislation which has only just been passed; but we are not persuaded that there is any case for change at all. It is worth reminding ourselves just how far-fetched the examples have to be – mistaking a person for an ape and the like – in order to raise the issue of whether the law is committed to drawing distinctions without a significant moral difference. We take the view that reliance on such scenarios is an insufficiently sound basis for altering the established law.

3.66   We should not leave this discussion without also referring to Article 2 of the European Convention on Human Rights. Article 2(1) provides that everyone's right to life shall be protected by law. Article 2(2) provides, amongst other things, that deprivation of life "shall not be regarded as inflicted in contravention of [Article 2] when it results from the use of force which *is no more than absolutely necessary*: (a) in defence of any person from unlawful violence".[74]

3.67   The right enshrined in Article 2(1) has been described as "one of the most fundamental provisions in the Convention".[75] It places a positive duty on the State to take appropriate steps to safeguard the lives of those within its jurisdiction.[76] This includes a duty to put in place

> effective criminal-law provisions to deter the commission of offences against the person backed up by law-enforcement machinery for the prevention, suppression and sanctioning of breaches of such provisions.[77]

3.68   A case on the narrow issue of mistakes caused by voluntary intoxication has yet to reach the European Court of Human Rights in Strasbourg, but the position in English law where D mistakenly believed he or she was entitled to kill in self-defence or the defence of another has been considered.

---

[73] See para 2.60 above.

[74] Emphasis added.

[75] *McCann v United Kingdom* (1995) App No 18984/91, para 147; *Gul v Turkey* (2002) App No 22676/93, 34 EHRR 28, para 76.

[76] *Osman v United Kingdom* (1998) App No 23452/94, para 115.

[77] Above.

3.69 The European Court of Human Rights has accepted that there is no conflict between Article 2 and the English common law rule insofar as it allows D to be judged according to the facts he or she mistakenly believed existed at the relevant time, where there are "good reasons" for the mistake;[78] that is, where the use of force

> is based on an honest belief which is perceived, for good reasons, to be valid at the time but which subsequently turns out to be mistaken.[79]

3.70 If "good reasons" is a requirement for Article 2(1) compatibility when Article 2(2)(a) is relied on, as the Strasbourg jurisprudence suggests, then a rule which would allow D to avoid all criminal liability for killing another person, on the basis of a mistake brought about by voluntary intoxication, would no doubt be regarded as incompatible with Article 2. Of course, if English law were to be reformed in the way suggested by the critics of *Hatton*,[80] with different rules depending on whether or not an integral fault element is alleged, D would not avoid all liability because D would be convicted of manslaughter (if D would not have made the mistake if sober). It may be that a conviction for manslaughter, carrying a discretionary life sentence and the label "homicide", would be sufficient to defeat an argument, based on Article 2 incompatibility, that the criminal law does not provide adequate protection.

3.71 Whether or not a manslaughter conviction would suffice for Article 2 compatibility, the Strasbourg jurisprudence reinforces our own view that self-defence should not be construed too widely if relied on to justify or excuse the deliberate taking of another person's life. D should not be able to avoid criminal liability for murder if his or her mistaken understanding of the facts was caused by voluntary intoxication.

3.72 It is important to add that the law governing self-defence is already extremely favourable to D because, as a general rule, the circumstances in which D acted must be taken to be those which D honestly believed to exist, even if no reasonable person could have had such a belief. We believe that to extend the basis of this defence to encompass mistakes caused by voluntary intoxication would be unwarranted, if not contrary to the State's duty under Article 2.

---

[78] For the common law rule, that D is entitled to rely on an honest mistake as to the facts when claiming he or she acted in self-defence, see *Williams (Gladstone)* (1983) 78 Cr App R 276 and *Beckford* [1988] AC 130. For the relevant Strasbourg jurisprudence, see, in particular, *McCann v United Kingdom* (1995) App No 18984/91, 21 EHRR 97, and *Gul v Turkey* (2002) App No 22676/93, 34 EHRR 28.

[79] *McCann v United Kingdom* (1995) App No 18984/91, 21 EHRR 97, para 200; *Gul v Turkey* (2002) App No 22676/93, 34 EHRR 28, para 78.

[80] [2005] EWCA Crim 2951, [2006] 1 Cr App R 16 (247).

3.73   We also find support for our view in the courts' approach to the common law defence of duress where, as in self-defence cases, D believes that he or she faces a threat of violence. If D wishes to rely on a factual mistake in seeking to establish duress,[81] and that mistake was attributable to voluntary intoxication, the mistake cannot be relied on.

3.74   We acknowledge that an old case[82] provides some support for the view that a mistake as to the facts caused by voluntary intoxication may nevertheless be relied on by D if he or she runs the (partial) defence of provocation to a charge of murder.

3.75   If this is still the law for provocation it runs contrary to the modern trend evidenced by the courts' approach to duress and self-defence. The retention of a special rule for provocation, if it can be described as such, is difficult to justify and would give rise to difficulties in cases where self-defence and provocation are run together as alternative defences to murder. We believe, therefore, consistent with our recommendation for self-defence, that, if D runs the defence of provocation on the basis that he or she mistakenly construed what was said or done by the deceased as provocative, and reacted accordingly with fatal consequences, D should not be able to rely on that mistake if it was caused by voluntary intoxication.

3.76   Our recommendation in paragraph 3.53 above therefore draws no distinction between the various defences. Putting aside the quite different case of insanity (which would continue to be governed by the common law),[83] D's mistaken belief as to the facts should be taken into account only if D would have held the same belief if D had not been intoxicated. This rule would apply to self-defence and section 3(1) of the Criminal Law Act 1967.[84] It would also apply, where relevant, to mistakes relied on in support of a partial defence to murder (diminished responsibility, provocation and suicide pact).

Example 3A

D is voluntarily intoxicated and, on the way home from a public house, he encounters another man (V) rapidly approaching him. Because of his intoxicated state, D mistakenly believes he is about to be attacked, and so grabs a piece of piping and strikes V intending to cause V serious harm before he himself suffers such harm. V is killed by the blow. It was D's intention to act lawfully in self-defence.

---

[81]   *Graham* [1982] 1 WLR 294, 300.

[82]   *Letenock* (1917) 12 Cr App R 221.

[83]   See paras 3.27 to 3.31 above and cl 9(4) of the new Criminal Law (Intoxication) Bill.

[84]   New Criminal Law (Intoxication) Bill, cl 5(2)(b) and (3)(b). Section 3(1) of the Criminal Law Act 1967 provides that a person "may use such force as is reasonable in the circumstances in the prevention of crime, or in effecting or assisting in the lawful arrest of offenders or suspected offenders or of persons unlawfully at large".

3.77 In determining D's liability for murder, the jury must consider D's actions in the circumstances as he would have understood them if he had not been voluntarily intoxicated. If D would not have made the same mistake if he had been sober, he would be liable for murder (because D killed V with the intention required for liability for murder). If it is plausible that D would have made the same mistake even if he had been sober, D would not be liable for murder (or manslaughter).

Example 3B

D is voluntarily intoxicated and, on the way home from a public house, he passes another man (V). Because of his intoxicated state, D mistakenly believes that V is criticising the appearance of his girlfriend and, provoked by the perceived slur, he grabs a piece of piping and strikes V intending to cause V serious harm. V is killed by the blow.

3.78 In determining D's liability for murder, the jury must consider D's actions in the circumstances as he would have understood them if he had not been voluntarily intoxicated. If D would not have made the same mistake if he had been sober, he would be liable for murder (because D killed V with the intention required for liability for murder and cannot rely on provocation to reduce his liability to manslaughter). If it is plausible that D would have made the same mistake even if he had been sober, D might be able to rely on the defence of provocation in answer to a murder charge.

3.79 Our recommendation in paragraph 3.53 above does not, however, apply to statutory provisions *framed* as defences which ostensibly require D to prove a non-culpable state of mind (an absence of culpable belief) if the courts have held that the provision in question should be regarded as one describing the absence of a fault element, and that it is for the prosecution to prove that fault element.[85] In such cases the culpable state of mind would be regarded as a fault element covered by the *Majewski* rule[86] or the rule for integral fault elements (as the case may be).[87]

Recommendation 5 ("honest belief" provisions)

3.80 **The rule governing mistakes of fact relied on in support of a defence (recommendation 4) should apply equally to "honest belief" provisions which state how defences should be interpreted.[88]**

---

[85] See, eg, *Lambert* [2001] UKHL 37, [2002] 2 AC 545 and *Lang* [2002] EWCA Crim 298 on s 28(2) and (3) of the Misuse of Drugs Act 1971.

[86] Paragraph 3.35 above.

[87] Paragraph 3.42 above.

[88] New Criminal Law (Intoxication) Bill, cl 5(5). See also cl 8(1).

3.81   In *Jaggard v Dickinson*[89] the Divisional Court held that where D is charged under section 1(1) of the Criminal Damage Act 1971,[90] the *Majewski* rule on self-induced intoxication does not apply to the statutory defence of lawful excuse set out in section 5(2). The reason given was that section 5(3) states that nothing more is required than an honest belief.[91] It was therefore irrelevant whether D's mistaken belief arose from a state of self-induced intoxication or any other unreasonable cause.

3.82   The judgment in *Jaggard v Dickinson*[92] is contrary to principle and contrary to the approach we recommend for defences generally. We also believe that the judgment was an erroneous interpretation of section 5(3) of the 1971 Act, given that Parliament presumably intended that the rule – subsequently the *Majewski* rule – governing intoxication and offences of "basic intent" would apply to the subsection. Our recommendation, which follows the Draft Criminal Code Bill and a recommendation made by the Commission in the 1995 report,[93] would reverse the Divisional Court's judgment and bring consistency to the law governing self-induced intoxication and defences.

3.83   Thus, suppose D is charged with criminal damage and wishes to rely on a defence in section 5(2) of the Criminal Damage Act 1971 on the basis that he or she made a genuine mistake as to the factual circumstances. In accordance with our present recommendation, if D's mistaken belief was induced by voluntary intoxication D would be regarded as not having had that belief if he or she would not have had it if sober (that is, if D had not been voluntarily intoxicated).

Recommendation 6 (negligence and no-fault offences)

3.84   **If the offence charged requires proof of a fault element of failure to comply with an objective standard of care, or requires no fault at all, D should be permitted to rely on a genuine but mistaken belief as to the existence of a fact, where D's state of mind is relevant to a defence, only if D would have made that mistake if he or she had not been voluntarily intoxicated.**

3.85   D's state of mind might be relevant to whether D is guilty of an offence of objective fault or a no-fault offence, even though the definitional elements of the offence do not make reference to D's state of mind. This is because D, charged with an offence of objective fault or a no-fault offence, may be able to avail him or herself of a *defence* to which his or her state of mind is relevant.

---

[89]   [1981] 1 QB 527, paras 2.94 to 2.96 above.

[90]   It is an offence under s 1(1) to destroy or damage property belonging to another person.

[91]   D relied on s 5(2)(a), which provides a defence if D "believed that the person or persons whom he believed to be entitled to consent to the destruction of or damage to the property in question had so consented, or would have so consented ... ". Section 5(3) provides that, for the purposes of s 5, "it is immaterial whether a belief is justified or not if it is honestly held".

[92]   [1981] 1 QB 527.

[93]   Legislating the Criminal Code: Intoxication and Criminal Liability (1995), Law Com No 229, paras 7.17 and 7.18.

> **Example 3C**
>
> D is charged with common assault and dangerous driving on the ground that he or she deliberately drove at a person V. The defence claim that D drove at V because of a mistaken belief that V was about to attack Y and that, accordingly, D was acting lawfully in accordance with the common law defence of self-defence (including defence of another) and/or the equivalent statutory defence provided by section 3(1) of the Criminal Law Act 1967.[94]

3.86 In this example, if D wishes to rely on a mistaken understanding of the facts in support of his or her defence, and D was voluntarily intoxicated at the time, D should be able to rely on the mistake only if D would have made the same mistake if he or she had been sober.[95]

3.87 Our new draft Criminal Law (Intoxication) Bill does not, however, restate the present law governing the relevance (or, rather, the irrelevance) of voluntary intoxication to the question whether the elements of an alleged no-fault offence or an offence of (gross) negligence can be proved.[96]

Specific recommendations for those who assist or encourage crime

Introduction

3.88 In two recent reports, *Inchoate Liability for Assisting and Encouraging Crime* (Law Com No 300 (2006)) and *Participating in Crime* (Law Com No 305 (2007)), we made a number of recommendations relating to the criminal liability of a person (D) who encourages or assists some other individual (P) to commit a crime (which, in the case of inchoate liability, would not actually need to be committed for D to be liable). Our recommendations for inchoate liability – the creation of new offences to cover persons who encourage or assist others to commit crime, whether or not the intended or contemplated crime is committed – have been taken forward by Parliament, albeit with some important changes, as Part 2 of the Serious Crime Act 2007.

---

[94] See fn 84 above.

[95] New Criminal Law (Intoxication) Bill, cl 5(2)(b) and (3)(b). Clause 5 would operate in this type of case because, as a provision in Part 2 of the Bill, it applies generally and is not limited in its application to offences defined with a subjective fault element.

[96] See fn 43 above.

3.89   We now consider the relevance of voluntary intoxication to cases of alleged secondary liability, as the law now stands, and cases of alleged assisting or encouraging under Part 2 of the Serious Crime Act 2007. In relation to secondary liability, we are concerned with allegations that D did not perpetrate the offence charged but is secondarily liable for it on the ground that he or she did "aid, abet, counsel or procure" the commission of the offence by another person, the perpetrator (P).[97] The fault element to be proved in such cases depends on whether or not it is alleged that D and P acted in concert as parties to a joint enterprise.

3.90   Where no joint enterprise is alleged, and D did not intend that the offence should be committed, it would appear that the prosecution must prove that D knew or believed that P would commit the offence (or that P was in the process of committing it), although the case law is not consistent.[98]

3.91   In cases where a joint enterprise is alleged, D may be convicted of an offence committed by P in relation to the enterprise if D was merely aware of the *possibility* that it would be committed.[99]

Recommendation 7 (secondary liability generally)

3.92   **For the doctrine of secondary liability generally (where no joint enterprise is alleged):**

   (1)   **if the offence is one which always requires proof of an integral fault element,[100] then the state of mind required for D to be secondarily liable for that offence should equally be regarded as an integral fault element;**

   (2)   **if the offence does not always require proof of an integral fault element,[101] then the (*Majewski*) rule on voluntary intoxication should apply in determining D's secondary liability for the offence.[102]**

---

[97]   Accessories and Abettors Act 1861, s 8; Magistrates' Courts Act 1980, s 44(1). The applicable rules determining D's liability comprise the common law doctrine of secondary liability (fn 12 in Part 1 above).

[98]   The older authorities on the question, which should be binding, suggest that if D does not intend the commission of P's offence there must be a requirement of "knowledge" (in reality a belief that P's offence will be committed); see *NCB v Gamble* [1959] 1 QB 11, *Johnson v Youden* [1950] 1 KB 544 and *Bainbridge* [1960] 1 QB 129. However, recent case law provides a degree of support for the proposition that the test is one of contemplation (eg, *Blakely and Sutton v DPP* [1991] RTR 405, 414 ("would, or might") and *Webster* [2006] EWCA Crim 415 ("likely to")). See generally Law Com No 305 (2007), Participating in Crime, pp 206 to 211.

[99]   Paragraph 2.98 above.

[100]   As opposed to an offence such as battery, which may be committed intentionally or recklessly.

[101]   For example, battery, which may be committed intentionally or recklessly.

[102]   New Criminal Law (Intoxication) Bill, cl 4.

3.93   One might be forgiven for believing that the state of mind required for secondary liability (without reference to the position for joint enterprises) should always be treated as an integral fault element unaffected by the *Majewski* rule. This, it would be argued, is because the prosecution's obligation to prove that D knew or believed that P would commit the offence, or that P was in the process of committing it, is akin to the state of mind we say should be an integral fault element for anyone charged with perpetrating an offence.[103]

3.94   However, in our view the state of mind required for secondary liability should be regarded as an integral fault element only if the offence committed by P requires proof of an integral fault element.[104] An example would be murder, which always requires proof of an intention to kill or cause grievous bodily harm.[105] If D is charged with being an accessory to P's offence of murder, and D was voluntarily intoxicated at the relevant time, D would not be liable for murder if D did not have the required culpable state of mind for secondary liability on account of his or her intoxicated state.

3.95   But if D is charged with being an accessory to P's offence of battery (an offence which may be committed intentionally or recklessly) the state of mind the prosecution would have to prove to secure a conviction for D would not be an integral fault element, regardless of how the allegation against P is framed. In such cases the general *Majewski* rule would apply in determining D's liability.[106] We believe that if recklessness is a sufficient basis for determining P's liability for battery, and P could therefore be convicted by the application of the *Majewski* rule as it applies to alleged perpetrators, it should also be possible to determine D's liability for the same offence on the same basis.

3.96   The contrary approach suggested in paragraph 3.93 above would limit the scope of the *Majewski* rule to an undesirable extent. Adopting this approach, the state of mind to be proved for secondary liability for an offence committed by P would always be an integral fault element even if the offence committed by P is defined in terms of recklessness, negligence or no fault. Such a difference in the rules to be applied, depending on whether it is alleged that the accused was a perpetrator or an accessory, would be difficult to justify.

---

[103] Paragraph 3.46(2) and (3) above.

[104] New Criminal Law (Intoxication) Bill, cl 4(4) and (5).

[105] Paragraph 1.13(1) above.

[106] New Criminal Law (Intoxication) Bill, cl 4(3).

3.97 In that regard, another reason for our recommendation is that it would be extremely unhelpful if different rules on the relevance of intoxication were to be created depending on whether it is alleged that the accused was a perpetrator or a secondary party. The approach we recommend would minimise the difficulties which might arise in a case where two persons are tried together on the basis that one was D (the accessory) and one was P (the perpetrator), but it is not clear who had which role. The jury could still be directed that it could convict both co-defendants of the offence on the basis that one of them was D and one of them was P.[107] This is because the rules governing the relevance of voluntary intoxication to criminal liability would be the same.[108]

3.98 An alternative approach, which would hold that the subjective fault for secondary liability is an integral fault element if the allegation against P is framed to require proof of an integral fault element, but not otherwise, would be more acceptable. However, it could give rise to real difficulties as P may never be charged (or even found) and P's state of mind may never be known.[109] Our recommendation avoids this problem.

Recommendation 8 (secondary liability – joint enterprises)

3.99 **Our proposed rule on the relevance of voluntary intoxication to secondary liability generally should apply equally to cases of alleged joint enterprise.[110]**

3.100 We have already explained that the *Chan Wing Siu* state of mind required for secondary liability in cases of joint enterprise, where D did not intend that the offence committed by P should be committed, is superficially similar to the concept of subjective recklessness.[111] This is because both culpable states of mind require the foresight of a possible eventuality which does not deter D from pursuing his or her hazardous conduct. If the *Chan Wing Siu* state of mind were to be regarded as a form of recklessness, D could be liable for murder committed by P on the basis that he or she did not foresee the possibility that P would commit murder but would have done if he or she had not been voluntarily intoxicated.[112]

---

[107] A permissible direction because the liability of a perpetrator and an accessory is the same. They are both guilty of the offence and liable to be punished to the same extent; see *Giannetto* [1997] 1 Cr App R 1.

[108] A problem might arise, exceptionally, if the prosecution were to frame the allegation of perpetrating an offence such as battery with reference to intention alone, but this is extremely unlikely.

[109] D may be convicted of an offence committed by P even if P is never found or prosecuted.

[110] New Criminal Law (Intoxication) Bill, cl 4. Clause 4 does not draw any distinction between the ways in which D may be secondarily liable for an offence perpetrated by P.

[111] See paras 2.98 to 2.101 above.

[112] The trial judge's summing up in *English* [1999] 1 AC 1 (p 27) suggests that the jury were directed to take D's intoxicated state of mind into account as a factor bearing on his secondary liability for murder, indicating that some judges already regard the *Chan Wing Siu* state of mind as a "specific intent" if it relates to an offence of "specific intent".

3.101   To treat the *Chan Wing Siu* state of mind as if it were a form of "recklessness" would be to establish an unacceptably broad basis for holding a person (D) liable for murder, given that for a perpetrator (P) to be convicted of murder the prosecution must prove that he or she killed with the intention to kill or cause grievous bodily harm.

3.102   In addition, we have already explained that, for secondary liability generally, the state of mind required on the part of D should be regarded as an integral fault element only if the offence charged (and allegedly committed by P) always requires proof of an integral fault element. We would not wish to create rules on the relevance of voluntary intoxication to secondary liability which differ depending on how the prosecution frames its case against D; and, as explained above,[113] we would not wish to create any distinction which would adversely affect the present rule whereby the accused can be convicted of an offence when it is proved that he or she was either the perpetrator or an accessory, but it cannot be proved which.

3.103   It follows, then, that the *Chan Wing Siu* state of mind for secondary liability for an offence committed by P should be treated as an integral fault element if P's offence always requires proof of an integral fault element.[114] But if P's offence can be committed intentionally or recklessly, and P's liability can be determined by the application of the *Majewski* rule, then the same rule should apply to D.

Recommendation 9 (inchoate liability)

3.104   **If D is charged under Part 2 of the Serious Crime Act 2007 with an offence of encouraging or assisting another person to commit a crime ("the crime"), then if the crime is one which would always require proof of an integral fault element for a perpetrator to be liable, and the allegation against D requires the prosecution to prove that D was "reckless" for the purposes of section 47(5) of the Act, the state of mind of being "reckless" should be treated as an integral fault element.[115]**

3.105   Part 2 of the Serious Crime Act 2007[116] takes forward proposals in the Commission's 2006 Report, Inchoate Liability for Assisting and Encouraging Crime (Law Com No 300), by creating new offences of encouraging or assisting crime.[117] These offences cover individuals who provide encouragement or assistance with the intention of encouraging or assisting the commission of a crime[118] or in the belief that a crime will be committed.[119]

---

[113] Paragraph 3.97.

[114] This may already be the law; see fn 112 above.

[115] New Criminal Law (Intoxication) Bill, cl 3(5)(e) and (6).

[116] The relevant provisions came into force on 1 October 2008; see The Serious Crime Act 2007 (Commencement No 3) Order 2008 (SI 2008 No 2504).

[117] Sections 44 to 46.

[118] Section 44.

[119] Principally s 45 (but also s 46).

3.106 These offences are inchoate offences. This means that, unlike the situation where the doctrine of secondary liability arises, D may be liable for encouraging or assisting a crime even if the crime in question is never committed and even if no-one other than D intended that it should be committed. Where D faces an allegation under section 45 (or section 46) that he or she encouraged or assisted a crime in the belief that it would be committed, it may be the case that the crime was never committed and that no-one, not even D, intended that it should be committed. Nevertheless, it must always be proved that D did an act (or failed to exercise a duty to act) which had the capacity to encourage or assist the commission of the relevant crime.

Example 3D

D provides P with a knife believing that P will use it to attack V.

3.107 In this example D could be charged with the offence of encouraging or assisting murder contrary to section 45 of the 2007 Act. This would require proof that D did an act capable of assisting P[120] to commit murder (in this scenario, the provision of the knife) and that D believed that:

(1) the *conduct* element of murder *would* be committed by P with the knife;[121]

(2) P *would or might* so act with the fault required for murder;[122] and

(3) V *would or might* die as a result.[123]

3.108 The view we took in Law Com No 300 was that factors (2) and (3) should not be satisfied unless it could be proved that D believed that P *would* act with the fault for murder and that V *would* be killed. However, the 2007 Act includes an alternative test of being "reckless" as to:

(1) P's fault;

(2) the consequence requirement of the offence (if any); and

(3) the circumstance requirement of the offence (if any).[124]

---

[120] For ease of exposition, reference is made here to another person "P", but the legislation does actually not require that D had a particular individual in mind.

[121] Section 47(3).

[122] Section 47(5)(a).

[123] Section 47(5)(b).

[124] See s 47(5)(a)(ii) and (b)(ii).

3.109   We recommended a narrower fault requirement because of the inchoate nature of D's liability, as explained above, and because the external element of D's offence would be satisfied by conduct which *could* encourage or assist the commission of the relevant crime.[125] It is to be noted that, because there is no requirement that the relevant crime must have been committed for D to be liable under the 2007 Act, there is no requirement that D must actually have encouraged or assisted the commission of the relevant crime.

3.110   Given the requirement under the 2007 Act of "recklessness", when the question of voluntary intoxication is brought into the equation D could, in the absence of an exception to the application of the *Majewski* rule, be liable for an offence of encouraging or assisting a substantive offence (including an offence requiring proof of an integral fault element) even though:

   (1)   the substantive offence was never committed;

   (2)   no harm was ever caused;

   (3)   no-one ever intended that the offence should be committed; and

   (4)   the basis of D's liability (other than D's belief that P would commit the conduct element with his or her assistance) is an imputed belief as to the *possibility* of fault (on the part of P) and/or the consequence and/or circumstance elements (relating to P's conduct).

3.111   We say this because the term "reckless" has been expressly used in section 47 to explain D's state of mind in relation to the elements of the relevant offence, and, both at common law and under our general rule[126] for alleged perpetrators,[127] the concept of being reckless is *not* an integral fault element.

3.112   Thus, in example 3D above, where D provides P with a knife, in the absence of an exception to the application of the *Majewski* rule D could be liable for the offence of encouraging or assisting murder even if, on account of voluntary intoxication, D did *not* envisage the possibility that P would act with the intention to kill or cause grievous bodily harm and did *not* believe that V might be killed, so long as D *would* have had those beliefs if he or she had not been voluntarily intoxicated.

3.113   It is perhaps true to say that D's conduct and state of mind in the example given will rarely come to the attention of the police unless P actually commits the anticipated offence. It may also be the case that the issue of intoxication will arise only rarely in this context.

---

[125] Compare the doctrine of secondary liability (Part 1, fn 12 above). Broadly speaking this doctrine requires that P, the perpetrator, committed the relevant offence with D's *actual* encouragement or assistance.

[126] New Criminal Law (Intoxication) Bill, cl 3(3).

[127] D is an alleged perpetrator, as opposed to a secondary party, if charged with an offence under the 2007 Act, although his or her liability is inchoate.

3.114   Nevertheless, we believe it would be wrong in principle to treat the concept of "reckless" in Part 2 of the 2007 Act as anything other than an integral fault element, if the offence D allegedly assisted or encouraged is one which always requires proof of an integral fault element.

3.115   It is worth repeating the important point made earlier with reference to secondary liability, that the word "reckless" in the context of Part 2 of the 2007 Act describes something quite different from the concept of recklessness as it is has traditionally been understood.[128] D's state of mind in the 2007 Act relates to the contemplated conduct of another person rather than D's own behaviour. So, if anything, it is analogous to the state of mind required for secondary liability in the context of a joint enterprise, a state of mind we have already explained should be treated as an integral fault element if the prosecution would always need to prove an integral fault element to convict a perpetrator.

3.116   The approach we now recommend for inchoate liability under the 2007 Act is one which would be consistent with the approach we have set out above for the doctrine of secondary liability.[129] Indeed, given our view that the joint enterprise *Chan Wing Siu* (foresight of a possibility) state of mind should be regarded as an integral fault element for secondary liability, in a case where the contemplated crime is actually committed by P (with D's encouragement or assistance), it would be quite wrong if the *Majewski* rule were to be applied to the *inchoate* bases of liability described by the provisions in the 2007 Act.

3.117   The consistency we recommend as between secondary and inchoate liability for encouraging or assisting crime would also mean that the jury would be directed in the same way as to the relevance of voluntary intoxication should D be charged as an accessory to P's crime, and charged in the alternative under the 2007 Act.[130]

3.118   Before leaving the area of inchoate liability we should add a comment on the offences of attempt and conspiracy, which we mentioned briefly in paragraphs 2.106 to 2.111 above.

3.119   In our recent consultation paper on attempt and conspiracy[131] we recommended that recklessness as to a circumstance should continue to be sufficient for attempt if it is sufficient for the completed substantive offence.[132] Equally, for the reasons given in paragraphs 2.109 to 2.110, we believe that the *Majewski* rule should apply to recklessness as to a circumstance in both types of case. Accordingly, we do not make any recommendation in this Report that recklessness where required for attempt should be regarded as an integral fault element which must always be proved.

---

[128] Paragraphs 2.99 to 2.100 above.

[129] Paragraphs 3.92 to 3.103 above.

[130] This could happen if the relevant substantive offence was committed by P but it was unclear whether D's conduct provided P with actual encouragement or assistance.

[131] Law Com Consultation Paper No 183 (2007), Conspiracy and Attempts.

[132] Above, paras 14.42 to 14.43.

3.120 There is currently no scope for the application of the *Majewski* rule to the offence of conspiracy because recklessness as to a circumstance does not suffice for liability where conspiracy is alleged. However, if the law were to be altered so that proof of recklessness as to a circumstance becomes sufficient for conspiracy where it is sufficient for the agreed substantive offence, in line with the proposal in our Consultation Paper No 183,[133] then it will be necessary to consider whether the *Majewski* rule should apply to this aspect of the requirements for conspiracy. This is a matter we will address in our forthcoming report on conspiracy and attempts.

RECOMMENDATIONS (2) – INVOLUNTARY INTOXICATION

Specific recommendations

Recommendation 10 (the general rule)

3.121 **D's state of involuntary intoxication should be taken into consideration:**

    (1)   in determining whether D acted with the subjective fault required for liability, regardless of the nature of the fault element;[134] and

    (2)   in any case where D relies on a mistake of fact in support of a defence to which his or her state of mind is relevant.[135]

3.122 This recommendation restates the common law position, explained in paragraphs 2.75 to 2.77 above, and little more needs to be said about it here. Of course, D's state of involuntary intoxication should also be regarded as an external agent for the purposes of the defence of automatism (that is, D should be able to rely on the defence if D's state of automatism resulted from his or her being involuntarily intoxicated). However, in accordance with our policy that the new draft Criminal Law (Intoxication) Bill should not address every factual scenario involving intoxication, this is an area which would continue to be governed by the common law.[136]

3.123 Although we do not recommend a statutory definition of "intoxicant" or "voluntary intoxication",[137] and no such definitions are provided in our new draft Bill, we believe that the concept of involuntary intoxication, or at least the most obvious situations which should be regarded as involuntary intoxication, should be expressly set out.[138]

---

[133] Above, para 4.113.

[134] New Criminal Law (Intoxication) Bill, cl 2.

[135] New Criminal Law (Intoxication) Bill, cl 5(3)(a).

[136] New Criminal Law (Intoxication) Bill, cl 9(4).

[137] Paragraph 3.25 above.

[138] In our new Criminal Law (Intoxication) Bill two situations are listed as "examples" on the ground that they are indeed obvious examples of involuntary intoxication (see cl 6(4)). Two other situations are listed separately (in cl 6(5)) because they are more akin to policy-driven rules than "examples".

3.124   If D's state of intoxication is not involuntary it would be regarded as voluntary.[139] This includes the situation where D feels compelled to become intoxicated on account of an addiction.[140]

Recommendation 11 (species of involuntary intoxication)

3.125   **There should be a non-exhaustive list of situations which would count as involuntary intoxication:**

(1)   **the situation where an intoxicant was administered to D without D's consent;**[141]

(2)   **the situation where D took an intoxicant under duress;**[142]

(3)   **the situation where D took an intoxicant which he or she reasonably believed was not an intoxicant;**[143]

(4)   **the situation where D took an intoxicant for a proper medical purpose.**[144]

3.126   **D's state of intoxication should also be regarded as involuntary if, though not entirely involuntary, it was *almost* entirely involuntary.**[145]

3.127   With regard to the recommendation in paragraph 3.126, intoxication which is partly voluntary and partly involuntary could be held to be involuntary intoxication if the voluntary aspect could be properly described as trivial when compared with the overriding impact of the involuntary aspect.

Example 3E

D's only pint of beer is surreptitiously laced with a hallucinogenic drug. If the self-induced aspect of D's state of intoxication was insignificant when compared with the extent to which D was involuntarily intoxicated then D would be regarded as involuntarily intoxicated.

---

[139] New Criminal Law (Intoxication) Bill, cl 6(1) and (2).

[140] New Criminal Law (Intoxication) Bill, cl 6(3).

[141] New Criminal Law (Intoxication) Bill, cl 6(4)(a).

[142] New Criminal Law (Intoxication) Bill, cl 6(4)(b).

[143] New Criminal Law (Intoxication) Bill, cl 6(5)(a).

[144] New Criminal Law (Intoxication) Bill, cl 6(5)(b).

[145] New Criminal Law (Intoxication) Bill, cl 6(1).

3.128   The various situations listed in paragraph 3.125 are mostly self-explanatory. In part they reflect the present law and in part they represent our view, informed by the conclusions in the 1995 report, of what the law ought to be.[146] The situation described in paragraph 3.125(4) does, however, require an explanation.

3.129   Save for one broad proviso, we believe that the situation where D takes an intoxicant for a proper medical purpose, as a type of involuntary intoxication, should be expressly limited to the taking of a properly authorised or licensed medicine or drug (for a proper medical purpose) in accordance with:

(1)   advice given by a suitably qualified person (such as a general practitioner or pharmacist);[147] and/or

(2)   the instructions accompanying the medicine or drug (such as a printed leaflet).[148]

3.130   We take the view that, if an untested (or improperly tested) "quack remedy" is taken according to the instructions provided with it, D should not be regarded as involuntarily intoxicated. The taking of an intoxicant in accordance with written instructions would be regarded as involuntary intoxication only if the intoxicant was a properly authorised or licensed medicine or drug. The question whether the intoxicant was a properly authorised or licensed drug or medicine would be a matter for the court to determine.

3.131   It is important to note that the approach we recommend would discard the unsatisfactory distinction which has been drawn at common law between dangerous and soporific drugs.[149]

3.132   The proviso mentioned in paragraph 3.129 is that D should be regarded as involuntarily intoxicated if D took a properly authorised or licensed medicine or drug (for a proper medical purpose) and, although D took it in a way which was not in accordance with advice given by a suitably qualified person or the instructions accompanying it, D ought nevertheless to be regarded as involuntarily intoxicated because, in the circumstances, it was *reasonable* for D to take the medicine or drug in that way.[150]

---

[146] Legislating the Criminal Code: Intoxication and Criminal Liability (1995), Law Com No 229, paras 8.9 to 8.35. See also s 6(5) of the Public Order Act 1986.

[147] New Criminal Law (Intoxication) Bill, cl 6(6)(a). Spurious advice given by an unqualified friend or colleague (or an unqualified medical practitioner) would not therefore be covered.

[148] New Criminal Law (Intoxication) Bill, cl 6(6)(b).

[149] Paragraphs 2.85 to 2.86 above (and see also fn 39 in Part 1 above).

[150] New Criminal Law (Intoxication) Bill, cl 6(6)(c).

3.133   This concession is flexible in nature. It provides D with an opportunity to avoid liability even though D would not ordinarily be regarded as involuntarily intoxicated. Given that no-one other than D is likely to have access to the relevant facts supporting or undermining his or her claim to reasonableness, we believe D should bear the burden of proving that it was reasonable for him or her to have done what he or she did.[151] This would require D to prove the factual circumstances he or she wishes to rely on in support of the claim to reasonableness.

3.134   We should add that we consider this broad, flexible approach to be more acceptable than a narrow alternative which would focus solely on the question whether, say, D foresaw the possibility that he or she would act in an aggressive or uncontrollable manner by not taking the medicine in accordance with medical advice or in accordance with the accompanying instructions.

Example 3F

D, a diabetic, takes a dose of insulin but fails to consume some food (as previously instructed by his doctor and/or the instructions accompanying the insulin), and thereby falls into a hypoglycaemic state during which D commits the external element of an offence requiring proof of subjective recklessness (contemplation of a risk). If D did not contemplate the risk D would otherwise have contemplated, D could be liable for the offence on the basis of being in a state of voluntary intoxication. However, D would be convicted on that basis only if D's conduct in not consuming sufficient food, contrary to the medical advice received or the instructions accompanying the insulin, was unreasonable in the circumstances.

3.135   Diabetes UK has indicated to us just how important it is not to treat diabetics who fail to maintain a normal blood glucose level through mismanagement of their condition as voluntarily intoxicated. The organisation said to us:

> The maintenance of near normal blood glucose is very difficult – some people manage it better than others. It requires doses of insulin or hypoglycaemic agents to be matched with food taken and activity. This will vary from person to person and according to different situations, for example stress or illness. Diabetes management is a balancing act between food intake, exercise, medication and life circumstances. There are so many variables that need to be taken into account that a person on insulin is inevitably going to have blood glucose levels above or below the normal range…

---

[151] New Criminal Law (Intoxication) Bill, cl 7(4).

3.136   The concession we recommend would ensure that a diabetic would be liable for an offence requiring proof of subjective recklessness only if his or her failure to maintain a normal blood glucose level was unreasonable. The question would be whether or not the conduct of the particular individual on trial was reasonable in all the circumstances.

RECOMMENDATIONS (3) – EVIDENCE AND PROOF

3.137   We have already set out our recommendation that D should have to prove the facts relied on in support of a claim that it was reasonable for him or her to take a drug or medicine in a way which was not in accordance with advice given by a suitably qualified person or the instructions accompanying it.[152] We also recommend the following rules relating to evidence and proof.

Additional specific recommendations

Recommendation 12 (prosecution alleges that D was intoxicated)

3.138   **If the prosecution alleges that D was voluntarily intoxicated at the material time:[153]**

(1)   **there should be a presumption that D was not intoxicated at the material time;**

(2)   **it should be for the prosecution to prove (beyond reasonable doubt) that D was intoxicated at the material time;**

(3)   **if it is proved (or admitted) that D was intoxicated, there should be a presumption that D was voluntarily intoxicated;**

(4)   **if D contends that he or she was involuntarily intoxicated, it should be for D to prove it (on the balance of probabilities).**

Recommendation 13 (D claims he or she was intoxicated)

3.139   **If D claims that he or she was intoxicated at the material time:[154]**

(1)   **there should be a presumption that D was not intoxicated at the material time;**

(2)   **D should bear an evidential burden in support of the claim that he or she was intoxicated at the material time;[155]**

---

[152] Paragraph 3.133 above.

[153] Because the offence, as alleged, requires proof of mere recklessness (or some other state of mind which is not an integral fault element).

[154] Because the prosecution are required to prove an integral fault element or D contends that he or she was involuntarily intoxicated.

[155] Given that the burden of proving that D was not intoxicated would lie with the prosecution (para 3.139(3) below) D would merely have to show there is admissible evidence suggesting intoxication as a plausible possibility.

(3) **if D's evidential burden is discharged (and the prosecution wishes to contend that D was not intoxicated), the prosecution should have to prove (beyond reasonable doubt) that D was not intoxicated;**

(4) **if D is taken to have been intoxicated, there should be a presumption that D was voluntarily intoxicated;**

(5) **if D contends that he or she was involuntarily intoxicated, it should be for D to prove it (on the balance of probabilities).**

3.140   Provisions which would give effect to these recommendations are set out in clause 7 of our new draft Bill.

3.141   The initial presumption that D was not intoxicated can be justified on the common sense basis that people are ordinarily sober and that, in the absence of any evidence of intoxication, the question does not warrant consideration.

3.142   The obligation on the prosecution to prove intoxication (beyond reasonable doubt) in a case where intoxication is alleged is right in principle, given that the prosecution will be wishing to circumvent its usual obligation to prove subjective recklessness (beyond reasonable doubt). In other words, if the prosecution alleges intoxication with a view to relying on the *Majewski* rule, the prosecution should have to prove the factual basis for the inapplicability of the rule.

3.143   The obligation on D to discharge a mere evidential burden on the issue, if D asserts that he or she was intoxicated at the material time, is also right in principle. It is right that some evidence should be adduced or elicited by D if D wishes to question, in relation to the facts of the instant case, the validity of the common sense presumption that D was sober. If the prosecution wishes to counter that D was not intoxicated, it is right in principle that the prosecution should prove its claim.

3.144   If it is proved or admitted, or to be presumed, that D was intoxicated at the material time, then as a matter of common sense there should be a presumption that D was voluntarily intoxicated. This is because intoxicated people, particularly those charged with criminal offences allegedly committed during their state of intoxication, are only very rarely involuntarily intoxicated.

3.145   Given the strength of this common-sense presumption of voluntary intoxication, if D wishes to claim that he or she was involuntarily intoxicated, we believe it is right that D should have to rebut the presumption by bearing the burden of proving involuntary intoxication on the balance of probabilities. It goes without saying that it could be extremely difficult for the prosecution to rebut the claim, if the prosecution were to be required to prove that D was not involuntarily intoxicated. We address this (reverse) burden of proof in more detail under the next heading.

THE HUMAN RIGHTS ACT 1998

3.146   Our recommended statutory version of the *Majewski* rule would continue to be a rule of substantive law and would not therefore engage Article 6 of the European Convention on Human Rights, which is concerned with procedural matters. This is now the established position in the light of the judgment of the House of Lords in *G*.[156]

3.147   It might be argued, however, that the rules we recommend which would place a burden of proof on D violate the presumption of innocence in Article 6(2) of the Convention.[157] We do not think the courts would accept this argument for several reasons.

3.148   The reasonableness provision we recommend for determining whether D's intoxication was involuntary where "proper medical purpose" is relied on,[158] and the general rule requiring D to prove involuntary intoxication in other cases,[159] would not require D to prove a defence let alone the absence of fault. D would merely need to prove the factual circumstances relied on in support of an argument that the *Majewski* rule for voluntary intoxication, a rule of the substantive criminal law, should not be applied; so it may well be that Article 6(2) is not even engaged.

3.149   In any event, even if Article 6(2) is engaged, we believe the reverse-burden provision in our draft Bill[160] would be held to be compatible with it as a reasonable measure directed at achieving a legitimate objective.

3.150   The circumstances D would wish to rely on when required to prove the reasonableness provision, or that D was otherwise involuntarily intoxicated, are likely to be circumstances D is best placed to establish and about which the prosecution would have very little or no information. If the reverse-onus provision were to be interpreted to place on D nothing more than an evidential burden, which could be easily discharged, thereby requiring the prosecution to prove that D was *not* involuntarily intoxicated, there would be a real possibility that the involuntary intoxication exemption from the *Majewski* rule would be removed by Parliament. This would place D in a worse position. It is to be noted that section 6(5) of the Public Order Act 1986 currently requires D to prove that his or her intoxication was involuntary.

3.151   Importantly, moreover, the prosecution would still need to prove beyond reasonable doubt that D committed the external element of the offence charged and:

   (1)   that D acted with the integral fault element alleged; or

---

[156] [2008] UKHL 37, [2008] 1 WLR 1379.

[157] "Everyone charged with a criminal offence shall be presumed innocent until proved guilty according to law."

[158] See para 3.133 above.

[159] See para 3.145 above.

[160] Clause 7(4).

(2)   if recklessness is alleged, and the presumption of voluntary intoxication applies, that D would have been aware of the relevant circumstances or risks if D had not been intoxicated.

3.152   The rule requiring D to prove that he or she was involuntarily intoxicated is based on the very strong common-sense presumption that criminal defendants who were intoxicated were voluntarily intoxicated. However, the rule would not require D to prove a defence or the absence of fault. So, again, if D cannot prove involuntary intoxication, the prosecution would still have to prove that D committed the external element of the offence charged with the integral fault element, where such fault is alleged; and, where recklessness is alleged, the prosecution would still have to prove that D would have been aware of all relevant circumstances or risks if D had not been intoxicated.

3.153   A rule placing the burden of proof on the prosecution, that is, a rule requiring the prosecution to prove beyond reasonable doubt that D was not involuntarily intoxicated once D had merely discharged an evidential burden on the issue, could be unworkable and, for that reason, might encourage many false claims of involuntary intoxication. As explained above, D is best placed to prove the extent and cause of his or her intoxication and it is difficult to see how the prosecution would be able to disprove beyond reasonable doubt a spurious claim of involuntary intoxication in many cases.

3.154   We should also briefly mention Article 7(1) of the European Convention, which provides, amongst other things, that no one "shall be held guilty of any criminal offence on account of any act or omission which did not constitute a criminal offence … at the time when it was committed".

3.155   In *SW v United Kingdom*[161] the European Court of Human Rights explained that the guarantee enshrined in Article 7(1) should be construed and applied "in such a way as to provide effective safeguards against arbitrary prosecution, conviction and punishment"[162] and is not limited to prohibiting the retrospective application of the criminal law. In particular, the guarantee requires that "an offence must be clearly defined in the law", a requirement which is satisfied "where the individual can know from the wording of the relevant provision and, if need be, with the assistance of the courts' interpretation of it, what acts and omissions will make him criminally liable".[163] Importantly, however, the Strasbourg court also accepted that Article 7 "cannot be read as outlawing the gradual clarification of the rules of criminal liability through judicial interpretation from case to case";[164] and it has been accepted by the Court of Appeal that there is no incompatibility for common law offences which develop incrementally.[165]

---

[161] (1995) App No 20166/92.

[162] Above, para 34.

[163] Above, para 35.

[164] Above, para 36.

[165] See *Clark* [2003] EWCA Crim 991, [2003] 2 Cr App R 23 (364).

3.156   Importantly, our recommendations do not bring any uncertainty to the scope or meaning of any criminal offence beyond that which already exists. That is to say, insofar as there might already be incompatibility by virtue of the fact that a statutory offence has an implicit requirement of subjective fault which the courts have not yet determined, our recommendations do not change the present position. The only difference introduced by our recommendations is that the courts would be aware, if they are not already aware, that the determination of the nature of any subjective fault element will be of relevance in a case where D is voluntarily intoxicated. This is because clause 3 of our new draft Bill expressly sets out which subjective fault elements are integral fault elements (which must always be proved)[166] and provides a general test for other subjective fault elements.[167]

FINAL COMMENT

3.157   In closing our analysis, we adopt the concluding remark of the Commission in the 1995 report:

> In practical terms ... the changes we propose would ... have the great merit of making the law consistent, coherent and much easier to apply, in cases where at present it is uncertain.[168]

3.158   It will be seen that our new draft Criminal Law (Intoxication) Bill appended to this report[169] reflects the current common law position in many respects and incorporates many of the recommendations made in the 1995 report.

3.159   If enacted, our new draft Bill would be complemented by the common law, with its in-built flexibility, to cover any situation where D was intoxicated and there is an issue of insanity or automatism.[170]

---

[166] New Criminal Law (Intoxication) Bill, cl 3(4) and (5).

[167] New Criminal Law (Intoxication) Bill, cl 3(3).

[168] Legislating the Criminal Code: Intoxication and Criminal Liability (1995), Law Com No 229, para 9.26.

[169] Appendix A.

[170] New Criminal Law (Intoxication) Bill, cl 9(4).

PART 4
INVOLUNTARY INTOXICATION AND CULPABILITY

4.1 It is trite law that, if D commits the external element of an offence with the required fault, then, subject to any defence he or she might have, D is liable for that offence.

4.2 In this Part we address the question whether D should be *excused* from liability, if his or her commission of an offence's external element with the required fault has been proved or admitted, on the basis that:

  (1) D's state of involuntary intoxication reduced D's inhibitions to such an extent that, although D was acting voluntarily and with the required fault, he or she could not resist the temptation to commit the offence charged; or

  (2) D's state of involuntary intoxication blurred D's moral vision to the extent that, although D acted with the required fault, appreciated what he or she was doing and could have acted otherwise, D did not appreciate the true moral gravity of his or her behaviour.

4.3 As the law stands, involuntary intoxication is not an excuse. Intoxication induced by the surreptitious act of a third party, for example, is irrelevant to the question of D's criminal liability if D acts with the fault required for liability, even if he or she would not have acted in that way if sober.

4.4 The law was definitively settled in the case of *Kingston*[1] where, reversing the decision of the Court of Appeal,[2] the House of Lords rejected the argument that reduced inhibitions brought about by involuntary intoxication resulting from the secret acts of a third party could be a defence at common law. K had committed indecent assault against a fifteen-year-old boy with the fault required for liability. He was therefore guilty of that offence even if it was accepted that he had abused the boy under the disinhibitive influence of a drug surreptitiously administered to him by his co-accused.[3]

4.5 Lord Mustill, in a speech with which the rest of the House agreed, reaffirmed the general principle that, unless relevant to a defence, the moral status or quality of an act does not affect its criminality, if it is proved that D committed the external element of a crime with the necessary fault. The degree to which D is or is not morally culpable for the offence committed is, and should continue to be, reflected only in the sentence handed down by the court.

---

[1] [1995] 2 AC 355.

[2] [1994] QB 81.

[3] As pointed out by the Court of Appeal in *Sheehan* [1975] 1 WLR 739, 744: "A drunken intent is nevertheless an intent."

4.6   Lord Mustill set out their Lordships' reasons for rejecting a general excuse of irresistible impulse, caused by involuntary intoxication, as follows:[4]

(1)   the existence of such a defence would be inconsistent with the common law position that an irresistible impulse having an internal origin (for which D is similarly not responsible) provides no defence if D acted with the required fault;

(2)   as a general defence available in respect of any offence, except perhaps offences not requiring fault, D would be able to avoid all liability, regardless of the seriousness of the offence;[5]

(3)   the defence would be inherently subjective, the sole question being whether D's inhibitions were in fact overcome by the drug;[6]

(4)   the defence would give rise to significant forensic problems, in that the jury would need to hear evidence of D's susceptibilities, and expert evidence would need to be called on the disinhibiting effect of a (quite possibly unknown) drug, or range of drugs, on those susceptibilities;

(5)   the defence would be easy to manufacture but difficult for the Crown to disprove; and

(6)   the involuntary nature of D's intoxication may be taken into consideration by the court as a mitigating factor when sentencing D for the offence he or she committed.

4.7   Lord Mustill suggested that the Law Commission might wish to enlarge its then project on intoxication to address the question. The Commission declined to accept this invitation, however, on the grounds that there had been no public consultation on the issue and the issue was in any event conceptually and practically different from the question whether a voluntarily intoxicated person should be liable if he or she has acted without the required fault.[7]

4.8   Given that we are now addressing the relevance of intoxication to criminal liability at large, we see no good reason for excluding the *Kingston* question from the scope of this Report. We therefore address the question in the following paragraphs. We recommend, however, that the common law position should be retained and, accordingly, that there should be no defence of reduced inhibitions or blurred perception of morality where D's condition was caused by involuntary intoxication.

---

[4]   [1995] 2 AC 355, 376 and 377.

[5]   The courts could, however, provide that the excuse is no defence to some of the most serious crimes, by analogy with the defence of duress.

[6]   Compare other excusatory defences, where reference is made to the reasonable person (albeit with D's relevant characteristics).

[7]   See Legislating the Criminal Code: Intoxication and Criminal Liability (1995), Law Com No 229, pp 2 and 3.

4.9   If created, a defence of reduced inhibitions or blurred moral vision would be relied on by D only in cases where it has been proved to the criminal standard that D committed the external element of the offence charged with the required fault. In our view, however, reduced inhibitions or blurred moral vision should have the effect, to a greater or lesser extent, of simply reducing the degree of blame that can be attached to D. In other words, evidence of involuntary intoxication in such cases should operate in the same way as do many (other) mitigating factors which were beyond D's power to control, such as a violent upbringing giving rise to an inability to control angry outbursts. With any like factor, D's involuntary intoxication may well justify a reduced sentence should he or she be convicted of an offence.

4.10   The justification given for the contrary position adopted by the Court of Appeal in *Kingston*[8] was its view that "the purposes of the criminal law are not served" by holding D liable when "the inhibition which the law requires has been removed by the clandestine act of a third party".[9] This approach accords with Professor Sullivan's (subsequently expressed) view that the law should take cognisance of D's lack of blameworthiness in such cases when attributing criminal liability.[10] However, we are unable to perceive any sufficient reason for elevating the mitigating factor of reduced inhibitions or blurred perception of morality caused by involuntary intoxication to the status of a new defence that would entirely negative D's criminal liability.

4.11   Another argument which might be raised in support of a complete defence of involuntary intoxication is that, as some other extraneous mitigating acts – duress by threats and duress of circumstances – already have the effect of completely excusing D's otherwise proven liability (albeit with some exceptions), so involuntary intoxication should similarly entitle D to an absolute acquittal.

4.12   Such an argument is sustainable only insofar as reduced inhibitions or blurred perceptions of morality may properly be regarded as analogous to the existing excusatory defences. There are, however, stark differences between the mere fact of reduced inhibitions or blurred perceptions of morality induced by involuntary intoxication and the duress defences. To rely on duress by threats, D must reasonably have believed, as a result of a threat, that death or serious injury would result if the offence was not committed; and it must be the case that a reasonable person (with D's relevant characteristics) would have committed the offence in those circumstances. Acting with fault but in a disinhibited or less morally aware state caused by surreptitiously administered drugs is far removed from the negation of culpability implicit in the defence(s) of duress.

---

[8]   [1994] QB 81, 89. According to the Court of Appeal, at p 89: "The law permits a finding that the intent formed was not a criminal intent or, in other words, that the involuntary intoxication negatives the fault element."

[9]   Above.

[10] GR Sullivan, "Making Excuses", Simester and Smith (eds) *Harm and Culpability*, p 131. Sullivan suggests an excusatory defence of involuntary intoxication for those of previous good character who have committed offences which do not involve death, serious injury or penetrative sexual acts.

4.13　There are, moreover, other extraneous circumstances which mitigate the culpability of the offender without affecting his or her criminal liability. For example, the fact that D was provoked into committing an offence is irrelevant to D's liability, regardless of how grievous the provocation was, unless D is charged with murder.[11] Provocative acts do not as a general rule affect D's liability, but are taken into consideration by the court only when passing sentence. It would be extremely difficult to justify a general excusatory defence of reduced inhibitions, obviating all liability, when it is accepted that the most grotesque acts of provocation cannot excuse liability for even relatively minor crimes.

4.14　The closest analogy with an existing complete defence is perhaps with insanity (of a temporary kind). However, the law does not permit the simple fact of blurred moral vision or moral disinhibition to amount to insanity in law.

4.15　There are also sound public policy reasons for rejecting a complete defence of reduced inhibitions or blurred moral vision founded on involuntary intoxication.

4.16　First, we agree that a defence of this sort would be too easy for the accused to manufacture. This would give rise to the very "disturbing prospect"[12] that the defence would be spuriously raised in any case where there was evidence that the accused was intoxicated at the time the offence was committed, particularly when it is remembered that so many offences of violence are committed under the influence of alcohol.

4.17　After all, D would need to do no more than call witnesses to say that he or she acted out of character, and give evidence, perhaps bolstered by similar evidence from his associates, that alcohol or some other drug must have been added to his (alcoholic or non-alcoholic) drink, causing his inhibitions to be reduced to the level at which he could no longer resist engaging in the offence. As Lord Mustill noted, the defence would be one which the Crown would often have no means of rebutting, and D would be entitled to an acquittal if it was reasonably possible that the defence was true.[13]

4.18　Reversing the burden of proof, that is, placing a legal obligation on D to prove the defence on the balance of probabilities, would make it more difficult for the defence to succeed. However, given the ease with which D would be able to fabricate evidence, the low standard of proof D would have to meet, and the problems the Crown would face in rebutting that evidence, there would still be considerable scope for successful reliance on an unmeritorious defence that allows culpable individuals to avoid all liability.

---

[11]　Successful reliance on this partial defence to murder results in liability for voluntary manslaughter and a discretionary life sentence.

[12]　*Kingston* [1995] 2 AC 355, 377, by Lord Mustill.

[13]　We do acknowledge, however, that it would be open to the Crown to explain to the jury that D's character evidence may be unreliable because of his or her personal relationship with the witnesses.

4.19   Secondly, the defence would be entirely subjective. The question would be whether D's personal inhibitions or moral compass, which ordinarily discourage D from committing the type of offence charged, were undermined as a result of involuntary intoxication to the extent that D should not be liable for that offence, even though D acted with the fault required for liability. There could be no "reasonable person" limb to the test because reasonable people do not have a latent disposition to commit crimes. For example, if the facts of *Kingston* were to recur, the jury would have to determine the inherent strength of D's particular sexual disposition towards adolescent boys and whether the degree to which he was affected by the intoxicant (the nature of which may be unknown) caused him, through his irresistible impulse or blurred awareness of morality, to commit an offence he would not otherwise have committed. It is questionable whether these are matters which expert witnesses would be able to throw much light on and, in the absence of relevant expert testimony, it is difficult to see how the jury could be expected to determine the question.

4.20   Thirdly, the stronger the accused's underlying but latent antisocial disposition, the easier it would be to rely successfully on the defence. If D has strong antisocial tendencies which can be kept under control when sober, but not when intoxicated, it would be relatively easy for D to demonstrate that the reduction in his or her inhibitions from the consumption of alcohol or some other drug is what caused the antisocial conduct on the occasion in question. The sole remaining issue would be whether or not the consumption was voluntary. Public safety requires that the strength of D's disposition to engage in antisocial conduct should not make it easier for D to claim a complete excuse for any crime committed in consequence.

4.21   Fourthly, if an excusatory defence were to be created for the situation where D's inhibitions are removed by an act for which he or she is not responsible, there would be little reason why the law should not recognise a general character-based excusatory defence for any inherent condition or "irresistible impulse" for which D is equally not responsible. For example, if D's urge to commit sexual offences against children is so great that he cannot withstand it, then logic would require that he too should be able to rely on the excuse of "insufficient inhibition" in relation to any sexual offence he commits against a child.[14] Indeed, if D has a disposition to behave in an antisocial way on account of the way he or she was raised during his or her formative years, again a matter beyond D's control, arguably there should also be an excuse from liability for that reason.

---

[14] It may be possible to rely on diminished responsibility as a partial (mitigating) defence if the allegation is murder.

4.22   There may well be an argument for introducing a general defence of diminished responsibility or provocation, or a broader defence of insanity, but these are matters beyond our present remit. In the absence of any such radical reform of the criminal law it would be illogical and anomalous to create a specific defence for persons whose inhibitions were affected by involuntary intoxication.[15]

4.23   In summary, the fact that the accused was involuntarily intoxicated at the time he or she committed the offence should normally be regarded as a mitigating factor, but it should not be elevated to the level of an excuse which would prevent any liability from attaching.

4.24   We agree with the view of Lord Mustill that:

> the interplay between the wrong done to the victim, the individual characteristics and frailties of the defendant, and the pharmacological effects of whatever drug may be potentially involved can be far better recognised by a tailored choice from the continuum of sentences available to the judge.[16]

4.25   The law is clear in the light of the House of Lords' judgment in *Kingston*[17] and, given our agreement with their Lordships' reasoning and approach, we make no recommendation for reform in this respect.

---

[15] For example, the involuntarily intoxicated paedophile who has committed an act of gross indecency against a young child would not be liable for his offence, notwithstanding the harm caused to the victim and proof of fault, but the child's mother, who found the paedophile in the act of committing the offence, and caused him serious non-fatal injuries as a result of her sudden and temporary loss of self control, would be liable for her very serious offence.

[16] *Kingston* [1995] 2 AC 355, 377.

[17] [1995] 2 AC 355.

PART 5
SUMMARY OF RECOMMENDATIONS

VOLUNTARY INTOXICATION

Recommendation 1: the *Majewski* rule

5.1   There should be a general rule that

(1)   if D is charged with having committed an offence as a perpetrator;

(2)   the fault element of the offence is not an integral fault element (for example, because it merely requires proof of recklessness); and

(3)   D was voluntarily intoxicated at the material time;

then, in determining whether or not D is liable for the offence, D should be treated as having been aware at the material time of anything which D would then have been aware of but for the intoxication.

[paragraph 3.35]

Recommendation 2: the rule for integral fault elements

5.2   If the subjective fault element in the definition of the offence, as alleged, is one to which the justification for the *Majewski* rule cannot apply, then the prosecution should have to prove that D acted with that relevant state of mind.

[paragraph 3.42]

Recommendation 3: the integral fault elements

5.3   The following subjective fault elements should be excluded from the application of the general rule and should, therefore, always be proved:

(1)   intention as to a consequence;

(2)   knowledge as to something;

(3)   belief as to something (where the belief is equivalent to knowledge as to something);

(4)   fraud; and

(5)   dishonesty.

[paragraph 3.46]

Recommendation 4 (defences and mistaken beliefs)

5.4 D should not be able to rely on a genuine mistake of fact arising from self-induced intoxication in support of a defence to which D's state of mind is relevant, regardless of the nature of the fault alleged. D's mistaken belief should be taken into account only if D would have held the same belief if D had not been intoxicated.

[paragraph 3.53]

Recommendation 5 ("honest belief" provisions)

5.5 The rule governing mistakes of fact relied on in support of a defence (recommendation 4) should apply equally to "honest belief" provisions which state how defences should be interpreted.

[paragraph 3.80]

Recommendation 6 (negligence and no-fault offences)

5.6 If the offence charged requires proof of a fault element of failure to comply with an objective standard of care, or requires no fault at all, D should be permitted to rely on a genuine but mistaken belief as to the existence of a fact, where D's state of mind is relevant to a defence, only if D would have made that mistake if he or she had not been voluntarily intoxicated.

[paragraph 3.84]

Recommendation 7 (secondary liability generally)

5.7 For the doctrine of secondary liability generally (where no joint enterprise is alleged):

(1) if the offence is one which always requires proof of an integral fault element, then the state of mind required for D to be secondarily liable for that offence should equally be regarded as an integral fault element;

(2) if the offence does not always require proof of an integral fault element, then the (*Majewski*) rule on voluntary intoxication should apply in determining D's secondary liability for the offence.

[paragraph 3.92]

Recommendation 8 (secondary liability – joint enterprises)

5.8 Our proposed rule on the relevance of voluntary intoxication to secondary liability generally should apply equally to cases of alleged joint enterprise.

[paragraph 3.99]

Recommendation 9 (inchoate liability)

5.9   If D is charged under Part 2 of the Serious Crime Act 2007 with an offence of encouraging or assisting another person to commit a crime ("the crime"), then if the crime is one which would always require proof of an integral fault element for a perpetrator to be liable, and the allegation against D requires the prosecution to prove that D was "reckless" for the purposes of section 47(5) of the Act, the state of mind of being "reckless" should be treated as an integral fault element.

[paragraph 3.104]

INVOLUNTARY INTOXICATION

Recommendation 10 (the general rule)

5.10   D's state of involuntary intoxication should be taken into consideration:

(1)   in determining whether D acted with the subjective fault required for liability, regardless of the nature of the fault element; and

(2)   in any case where D relies on a mistake of fact in support of a defence to which his or her state of mind is relevant.

[paragraph 3.121]

Recommendation 11 (species of involuntary intoxication)

5.11   There should be a non-exhaustive list of situations which would count as involuntary intoxication:

(1)   the situation where an intoxicant was administered to D without D's consent;

(2)   the situation where D took an intoxicant under duress;

(3)   the situation where D took an intoxicant which he or she reasonably believed was not an intoxicant;

(4)   the situation where D took an intoxicant for a proper medical purpose.

5.12   D's state of intoxication should also be regarded as involuntary if, though not entirely involuntary, it was *almost* entirely involuntary.

[paragraphs 3.125–3.126]

EVIDENCE AND PROOF

Recommendation 12 (prosecution alleges that D was intoxicated)

5.13   If the prosecution alleges that D was voluntarily intoxicated at the material time:

(1)   there should be a presumption that D was not intoxicated at the material time;

(2)   it should be for the prosecution to prove (beyond reasonable doubt) that D was intoxicated at the material time;

(3)   if it is proved (or admitted) that D was intoxicated, there should be a presumption that D was voluntarily intoxicated;

(4)   if D contends that he or she was involuntarily intoxicated, it should be for D to prove it (on the balance of probabilities).

[paragraph 3.138]

Recommendation 13 (D claims he or she was intoxicated)

5.14   If D claims that he or she was intoxicated at the material time:

(1)   there should be a presumption that D was not intoxicated at the material time;

(2)   D should bear an evidential burden in support of the claim that he or she was intoxicated at the material time;

(3)   if D's evidential burden is discharged (and the prosecution wishes to contend that D was not intoxicated), the prosecution should have to prove (beyond reasonable doubt) that D was not intoxicated;

(4)   if D is taken to have been intoxicated, there should be a presumption that D was voluntarily intoxicated;

(5)   if D contends that he or she was involuntarily intoxicated, it should be for D to prove it (on the balance of probabilities).

[paragraph 3.139]

(*Signed*)   TERENCE ETHERTON, *Chairman*
ELIZABETH COOKE
DAVID HERTZELL
JEREMY HORDER
KENNETH PARKER

WILLIAM ARNOLD, *Chief Executive*
4 December 2008

Appendix A - Draft Criminal Law (Intoxication) Bill and Notes

CONTENTS

PART 1

VOLUNTARY AND INVOLUNTARY INTOXICATION: BASIC RULES

PART 2

OTHER PROVISIONS

DRAFT

OF A

B I L L

TO

Make provision, subject to certain exceptions, about the effect of intoxication on criminal liability.

B E IT ENACTED by the Queen's most Excellent Majesty, by and with the advice and consent of the Lords Spiritual and Temporal, and Commons, in this present Parliament assembled, and by the authority of the same, as follows:—

PART 1

VOLUNTARY AND INVOLUNTARY INTOXICATION: BASIC RULES

1   Application and interpretation of Part 1

(1)   This Part applies where—
  (a)   there are proceedings against a person ("D") for an offence,
  (b)   D's liability for it requires proof of a fault element which depends upon D's state of mind,
  (c)   it is alleged that the fault element was present at any material time, and
  (d)   at that time D was intoxicated.

(2)   In subsection (1), references to a fault element include any fault element which the prosecution must prove (regardless of how the offence is defined), except one which arises when either of the following issues is raised—
  (a)   whether or not D is entitled to rely on the common law defence of self-defence,
  (b)   whether or not D used reasonable force for the purposes of section 3(1) of the Criminal Law Act 1967 (c. 58) (use of force in making arrest etc.).

(3)   In this Part—
  (a)   "D" is the person referred to in subsection (1),
  (b)   "the allegation" means the allegation referred to in subsection (1)(c),
  (c)   references to acts, and related expressions, include omissions and similarly related expressions.

EXPLANATORY NOTES

A.1 The Draft Bill, which would extend to England and Wales only,[1] is divided into two Parts:

- Part 1 applies only if the accused ("D") is charged with an offence, either as a perpetrator or as an accessory, and the prosecution has to prove that D acted with a requirement of subjective fault. (Part 1 comprises clauses 1 to 4.)

- Part 2 applies generally, so it also covers the situations where D is charged with an offence requiring proof of objective fault or an offence which does not require proof of any fault. (Part 2 comprises clauses 5 to 9.)

Clause 1

A.2 Clause 1(1) provides that in any case where D is charged with an offence, and the prosecution has to prove that D acted with subjective fault ("a fault element which depends upon D's state of mind")[2] to be convicted of it, then, if D was intoxicated at the time he or she allegedly committed the offence, the applicable provisions of Part 1 apply.[3]

A.3 Clause 1(2) provides that in determining whether the offence is one to which Part 1 applies the concept of subjective fault encompasses any culpable state of mind which the prosecution has to prove for D to be convicted.

A.4 It does not matter, therefore, whether:

- the offence has been expressly defined with reference to the culpable state of mind as a fault element to be proved by the prosecution, or

- the courts have held that a "defence" of no culpable state of mind is to be interpreted as a fault requirement to be proved by the prosecution (once D has discharged a mere evidential burden on the absence of such fault).[4]

A.5 Clause 1(2) also provides, however, that the defences in paragraphs (a) and (b) (the common law defence of self-defence and the similar defence in section 3(1) of the Criminal Law Act 1967) are not to be treated as a denial of the fault element, regardless of the theoretical position.[5] They are to be treated as "defences" covered by clause 5.[6]

---

[1] Save that one consequential amendment also extends to Northern Ireland; see clause 9(6) which must be read with clauses 8(3) and 9(5).

[2] Clause 1(1)(b).

[3] Clause 2 governs the situation where D's intoxication was involuntary. Clauses 3 and 4 govern the situation where D's intoxication was voluntary. Clause 3 applies if D is an alleged perpetrator. Clause 4 applies if D is an alleged accessory. Clause 6 provides the meaning of voluntary intoxication and involuntary intoxication. Clause 7 sets out a number of rules and presumptions relating to the question whether or not D was intoxicated and, if so, whether or not D's state of intoxication was voluntary or involuntary.

[4] See, eg, *Lambert* [2001] UKHL 37, [2002] 2 AC 545 on s 28 of the Misuse of Drugs Act 1971.

[5] Strictly speaking, if D successfully relies on self-defence (or s 3(1) of the Criminal Law Act 1967), D is regarded as having acted without the subjective fault element required for liability.

[6] See clause 5(2)(b).

2   Involuntary intoxication

If D's intoxication was involuntary, evidence of it may be taken into account in determining whether the allegation has been proved.

EXPLANATORY NOTES

Clause 2

A.6 Clause 2 sets out the rule that, in any case where the prosecution has to prove that D acted with an element of subjective fault to be liable for the offence charged, D's state of *involuntary* intoxication is to be taken into account in determining whether D acted with that state of mind.

A.7 In other words, if D did not act with the required subjective fault on account of being involuntarily intoxicated, then D is not liable for the offence charged.

3   Voluntary intoxication: liability of perpetrator

(1)   This section applies unless the proceedings against D are for aiding, abetting, counselling or procuring the commission of an offence (for which see section 4).

(2)   This section applies only if D's intoxication was voluntary.

(3)   Where this section applies, the general rule is that in determining whether the allegation has been proved, D is to be treated as having been aware at the material time of anything which D would then have been aware of but for the intoxication.

(4)   There are five cases in which the general rule does not apply: in those cases, evidence of D's intoxication may be taken into account in determining whether the allegation has been proved.

(5)   The five cases are that the allegation is, in substance, that at the material time—

    (a)   D intended a particular result (but this does not include merely intending to do the acts which constitute the conduct element of the offence),

    (b)   D had any particular knowledge as to something (but this does not include knowledge as to a risk),

    (c)   D had a particular belief, amounting to certainty or near-certainty, that something was then, had been, or would in future be, the case,

    (d)   D acted fraudulently or dishonestly,

    (e)   D was reckless for the purposes of subsection (5)(a)(ii) or (b)(ii) of section 47 of the Serious Crime Act 2007 (c. 27) (concerning proof for the purposes of that section that an act is one which, if done by another person, would amount to the commission of an offence by that other person).

(6)   Paragraph (e) of subsection (5) applies only if liability for the offence mentioned in that paragraph would (if there were proceedings against the other person for it) require proof of an allegation against that person which is of any kind mentioned in paragraphs (a) to (d) of that subsection.

EXPLANATORY NOTES

Clause 3

A.8 Clause 3(1) and (2) provides that clause 3 applies if D's state of intoxication was *voluntary* and it is alleged that D *perpetrated* the offence charged. Clause 3(3) then sets out the general rule for such cases: D is to be treated as having been aware of anything D would have been aware of if D had not been intoxicated. There are several exceptions to this general rule[7] and these are listed in clause 3(5).

A.9 Save for one specific proviso,[8] the fault element of recklessness is not included within clause 3(5), so subjective recklessness is governed by the general rule set out in clause 3(3): D is to be treated as if D had been aware of any risk D would have been aware of if D had not been intoxicated.

A.10 Clause 3(5) lists the types of subjective fault element which, if in issue, must always be proved by the prosecution, whether or not D was voluntarily intoxicated.[9] Paragraphs (a) to (d) list the following subjective fault elements: intention as to a result; knowledge as to something (other than a risk); belief amounting to certainty or near certainty as to something; fraud; and dishonesty. Paragraph (e), which must be read with clause 3(6), provides that the fault element of recklessness in section 47 of the Serious Crime Act 2007 is to be treated in the same way.

A.11 However, clause 3(6) sets out a special rule for the situation where the prosecution must prove that D acted recklessly for the purposes of section 47 of the Serious Crime Act 2007, where it is alleged that D encouraged or assisted the commission of another offence ("the offence mentioned in [paragraph (e)]"). The state of mind covered by the term "reckless" in this specific context is to be regarded as a fault element which must always be proved, rather than a fault element covered by the general rule in clause 3(3), but only if the offence mentioned in paragraph (e) is an offence which always requires proof of a state of mind falling within clause 3(5)(a) to (d).

A.12 Thus, if D is charged under the 2007 Act with encouraging or assisting murder and the prosecution alleges "recklessness" (within section 47), the prosecution must prove that D was indeed reckless.[10] But if D is charged with encouraging or assisting a battery, then an allegation of recklessness (within section 47) is governed by the general rule in clause 3(3).[11]

---

[7] See clause 3(4).

[8] Clause 3(5)(e) and (6).

[9] Clause 3(4) provides that "evidence of D's [voluntary] intoxication may be taken into account in determining whether the allegation has been proved".

[10] This is because the intention to kill or cause grievous bodily harm must always be proved if a person is charged with perpetrating murder (see clause 3(5)(a)).

[11] This is because battery can be committed intentionally or recklessly.

4   Voluntary intoxication: secondary liability

(1)   This section applies if the proceedings against D are (whatever expression is used) for aiding, abetting, counselling or procuring the commission of an offence by another person ("P").

(2)   This section applies only if D's intoxication was voluntary.

(3)   Where this section applies, the general rule is that in determining whether the allegation has been proved, D is to be treated as having been aware at the material time of anything which D would then have been aware of but for the intoxication.

(4)   There is one case in which the general rule does not apply: in that case, evidence of D's intoxication may be taken into account in determining whether the allegation has been proved.

(5)   The one case is that liability for the offence which D is said to have aided, abetted (etc.) would (if there were proceedings against P for it) require proof of an allegation against P which is of any kind mentioned in section 3(5)(a) to (d).

(6)   For the purposes of subsection (3) it does not matter—

(a)   whether the offence which D is said to have aided, abetted (etc.) has a fault element at all, or

(b)   if it does, what sort of fault element it is.

EXPLANATORY NOTES

Clause 4

A.13   Clause 4(1) and (2) provides that clause 4 applies if D's state of intoxication was *voluntary* and it is alleged that D is liable for the offence charged as an *accessory*. In other words, it is alleged that D is liable for an offence committed by a perpetrator (P) by the application of the general doctrine of secondary liability, or pursuant to a specific statutory provision, on the ground that D aided, abetted, counselled, or procured the commission of P's offence.[12] It is to be noted that no distinction is drawn between the general doctrine of secondary liability and the particular rules which apply to joint enterprises. All cases of alleged secondary liability are governed by clause 4. As explained above, however, the situation where D is charged with having encouraged or assisted the commission of another offence under Part 2 of the Serious Crime Act 2007 is governed by clause 3.[13]

A.14   Clause 4(3) sets out the general rule that D is to be treated as having been aware of anything which D would have been aware of if D had not been intoxicated.

A.15   By virtue of clause 4(4) and (5), however, a different rule applies if the offence committed by P is one which always requires proof of a culpable state of mind (on the part of P) falling within clause 3(5)(a) to (d). For offences of this sort, such as murder, the culpable state of mind required (on the part of D), to be convicted of P's offence as an accessory, is to be treated as a fault element which must always be proved. Where this rule applies, evidence of D's (voluntary) intoxication is to be taken into account in determining whether or not D acted with the required state of mind.[14]

A.16   Thus, if the offence committed by P is battery, which may be committed by P intentionally or recklessly, P's liability is to be established with reference to the general rule in clause 3(3). Equally, if D is charged with battery on the basis of the doctrine of secondary liability, the state of mind the prosecution must prove that D acted with is not to be regarded as an integral fault element. The same general rule applies to D by the application of clause 4(3).

A.17   If, however, it is alleged that D was an accessory to murder, an offence which always requires proof of an intention to kill or cause grievous bodily harm, then the general rule in clause 4(3) does not apply.[15] D can be convicted of murder only if D acted with the state of mind required by the doctrine of secondary liability to be liable for P's murder.

A.18   Clause 4(6) simply provides that the general rule in clause 4(3) extends to the situation where it is alleged that D is secondarily liable for an offence (committed by P) which does not require proof of subjective fault. This provision has been included because, under the doctrine of secondary liability, the prosecution may have to prove that D acted with subjective fault, in which case clause 4(3) applies, even though the offence committed by P has a requirement of objective fault or does not require proof of any fault.

---

[12]   With regard to the general doctrine of secondary liability, see s 8 of the Accessories and Abettors Act 1861 and s 44 of the Magistrates' Courts Act 1980. However, clause 4(1) is not limited to the situations where one of these provisions is relied on. This is because a number of other provisions provide, in effect, that D can be convicted of an offence on the basis that he or she encouraged or assisted the perpetrator to commit it, and the formula used may not follow the "aid, abet, counsel or procure" wording of the general provisions. See, for example, s 7(1) of the Perjury Act 1911.

[13]   Liability under Part 2 of the Serious Crime Act 2007 is not secondary liability for an offence committed by another person but primary liability for an offence committed by D.

[14]   Clause 4(4). This rule for secondary liability is therefore the same as the rule under clause 3(5)(e) and (6) for some cases where it is alleged that D encouraged or assisted an offence under Part 2 of the Serious Crime Act 2007.

[15]   Clause 4(4) and (5), read with clause 3(5)(a).

PART 2

OTHER PROVISIONS

5   Mistaken beliefs and intoxication

(1)   This section applies if —

    (a)   there are proceedings against a person ("D") for any offence,

    (b)   D was at any material time intoxicated, and

    (c)   by way of defence, or in support of a defence, D relies on having at that time held a particular belief as to any fact.

(2)   In this section, "defence" —

    (a)   does not include anything which, if raised as an issue, imposes the burden of proving a fault element falling within section 1(1) on the prosecution, but

    (b)   does include the defences referred to in section 1(2)(a) and (b).

(3)   In determining D's liability for the offence —

    (a)   if D's intoxication was involuntary, D's actual belief, whether mistaken or not, is to be taken into account, but

    (b)   if D's intoxication was voluntary, D's actual belief is to be taken into account only if D would have held the same belief if not intoxicated.

(4)   If evidence is adduced which is sufficient to raise an issue to the effect that D would have held the same belief if not intoxicated, it is to be taken that D would have held that belief unless the prosecution proves beyond reasonable doubt that D would not.

(5)   Any enactment or provision of subordinate legislation (whatever its terms) by virtue of which the holding of a particular belief provides, or supports, a defence to a criminal charge has effect subject to this section.

EXPLANATORY NOTES

Clause 5

A.19 Clause 5 sets out the position for mistakes induced by intoxication where D's state of mind is relevant to a *defence*:[16]

- If D's mistake was induced by involuntary intoxication, then D is to be judged according to his or her mistaken understanding of the facts (clause 5(3)(a));[17]

- If D's mistake was induced by voluntary intoxication, then D may rely on that mistaken belief only if D would have made the same mistake if D had not been intoxicated (clause 5(3)(b)).

A.20 Importantly, no distinction is drawn in clause 5(3)(b) between offences requiring proof of a clause 3(5) state of mind and other offences. Thus, in line with the position at common law and section 76(5) of the Criminal Justice and Immigration Act 2008, D may rely on a mistake as to the facts in support of the defence of self-defence only if D would have made the same mistake if he or she had been sober, even if the definition of the offence charged requires proof of a fault element falling within clause 3(5).[18]

A.21 It is also to be noted that, as a provision in Part 2, clause 5 applies generally. It is not limited to the situation where the prosecution has to prove that D acted with subjective fault to be liable for the offence charged. Clause 5 applies, therefore, if D wishes to rely on a defence (to which D's state of mind is relevant) to avoid being convicted of an offence which requires proof of objective fault or which does not require proof of any fault.

A.22 Clause 5(4) provides that D bears an evidential burden as to whether D would have had the same mistaken belief if he or she had not been voluntarily intoxicated but that, if D discharges the evidential burden, the burden of proof on the issue lies with the prosecution. This means that, so long as D can point to credible, admissible evidence suggesting that D might plausibly have made the same mistake if he or she had been sober, then the prosecution must prove beyond reasonable doubt that D would not have made the same mistake if sober.

A.23 By virtue of clause 5(5), these rules apply to all statutory provisions which provide that D's mistaken understanding of the facts amounts to, or is relevant to, a defence (as defined in clause 5(2)). Thus, to take a couple of examples, section 5(3) of the Criminal Damage Act 1971[19] and section 12(6) of the Theft Act 1968[20] must be read in accordance with clause 5(3)(b) if D's state of intoxication was self-induced.[21]

---

[16] Clause 5(1) and (2). An element which has been framed as a defence, but which the prosecution must prove as a *fault* element, is covered by clause 3 or clause 4 (see clause 1(1) and (2) with clause 5(2)(a)). The defences set out in clause 1(2)(a) and (b) are covered by clause 5 (clause 5(2)(b)).

[17] This is in line with clause 2.

[18] Clause 8(3) replaces s 76(5) of the Criminal Justice and Immigration Act 2008 so that the provisions of s 76 are read with the more general rules in clause 5 (with no change in the substance of the law governing intoxication and self-defence). Similarly, s 6(5) and (6) of the Public Order Act 1986 is repealed by clause 8(2) so that the position for s 6, where D is voluntarily intoxicated, is governed by the Bill's general provisions.

[19] The "honest belief" provision which may be relied on in support of a defence under s 5(2) of the Act.

[20] The "belief that he has lawful authority" defence to a charge of taking a conveyance without consent under s 12(1) of the Act.

[21] This reverses *Jaggard v Dickinson* [1981] 1 QB 527 in this respect. See also clause 8(1) which amends s 5(3) of the Criminal Damage Act 1971 to make the position clear beyond peradventure.

6   Meaning of voluntary and involuntary intoxication

(1)   For the purposes of this Act, an intoxicated person ("D") is involuntarily intoxicated if D's intoxication was entirely, or almost entirely, involuntary.

(2)   Otherwise, for the purposes of this Act D is voluntarily intoxicated.

(3)   If D's intoxication results from taking an intoxicant because of an addiction, it counts as voluntary.

(4)   Intoxication resulting from either of the following is an example of involuntary intoxication—

    (a)   administration of an intoxicant to D without D's consent,

    (b)   taking an intoxicant under duress.

(5)   If D's intoxication results from either of the following, it counts as involuntary—

    (a)   taking an intoxicant which D reasonably believed was not an intoxicant,

    (b)   taking an intoxicant for a proper medical purpose.

(6)   D is to be regarded as taking an intoxicant for a "proper medical purpose" only if it was a drug or medicine properly authorised or licensed by an appropriate authority and—

    (a)   D took it in accordance with the advice of a suitably qualified person, or

    (b)   D took it in accordance with the instructions accompanying it, or

    (c)   if D took it otherwise than as mentioned in paragraph (a) or (b), it was reasonable for D to have done so.

EXPLANATORY NOTES

Clause 6

A.24   Clause 6(1) provides that D is to be regarded as involuntarily intoxicated if the intoxication was entirely or almost entirely involuntary. Some cases where D is to be regarded as having been involuntarily intoxicated are set out in clause 6(4) and (5).[22]

A.25   Clause 6(2) provides that if an intoxicated D was not involuntarily intoxicated he or she is to be regarded as having been voluntarily intoxicated. Clause 6(3) provides that the taking of an intoxicant "because of an addiction" is to be treated as voluntary intoxication. Thus D, a heroin addict, who becomes intoxicated having taken heroin, will not be able to claim that his or her intoxication was involuntary.

A.26   Clause 6(4) sets out two examples of involuntary intoxication (administering an intoxicant without D's consent and taking an intoxicant under duress), but the list is not exhaustive.

A.27   Clause 6(5) provides, in addition, that D is to be treated as having been involuntarily intoxicated if D took the intoxicant in the reasonable belief that it was not an intoxicant or D took the intoxicant for a proper medical purpose. If D relies on the "proper medical purpose" basis for avoiding the rules applicable to cases of voluntary intoxication, it is necessary to refer to clause 6(6).

A.28   The general position for D who wishes to rely on "proper medical purpose" is set out in clause 6(6)(a) and (b); but if D did not comply with the requirements of paragraph (a) or (b) D will nevertheless be regarded as involuntarily intoxicated if D proves (on the balance of probabilities) that his or her conduct was reasonable in the circumstances.[23]

A.29   But what of the situation where D becomes addicted to an intoxicating drug which was originally prescribed for a proper medical purpose and, in a state of intoxication, D commits the external element of a crime? In a case of this sort the court would first need to consider whether the relevant taking of the drug was for a proper medical purpose within the requirements of clause 6(5)(b) and (6). If it was, then D's state of intoxication would be regarded as involuntary. If, however, the prescription was just part of the history, and D's taking of the drug was no longer for a proper medical purpose, then D's intoxication would be regarded as voluntary, notwithstanding the addiction.[24]

---

[22]   It is for D to prove that he or she was involuntarily intoxicated; see clause 7(4).

[23]   Clause 6(6)(c) and clause 7(4).

[24]   Clause 6(3).

7   Presumptions and proof

(1)   In this section, "D" means the person referred to in section 1(1) or 5(1).

(2)   For the purposes of this Act it is to be taken that D was not intoxicated at the material time, unless —

(a)   the prosecution proves the contrary beyond reasonable doubt, or

(b)   D adduces evidence which is sufficient to raise an issue to the contrary.

(3)   If D adduces evidence as mentioned in subsection (2)(b), it is to be taken for the purposes of this Act that D was intoxicated at the material time, unless the prosecution proves beyond reasonable doubt that D was not.

(4)   If for the purposes of this Act D was (or is to be taken to have been) intoxicated at the material time, then it is to be taken for those purposes that D's intoxication was voluntary, unless D shows the contrary on the balance of probabilities.

EXPLANATORY NOTES

Clause 7

A.30   Clause 7 sets out the rules governing the incidence of the burden of proof and the standard of proof to be applied in cases where intoxication arises as a potential issue.

A.31   Clause 7(2) provides, in effect, that it is to be presumed that D was not intoxicated at the relevant time. The provision goes on to provide, however, that either party may rebut the presumption:

- The prosecution will rebut this presumption of sobriety by proving that D was intoxicated.[25] The prosecution will seek to do this if reliance is to be placed on one of the general rules for voluntary intoxication and subjective fault (clause 3(3) and clause 4(3)) or the equivalent rule for defences (clause 5(3)(b)).[26]

- If D wishes to rely on clause 2, clause 3(4) and (5), clause 4(4) and (5), or clause 5(3)(a), D will seek to rebut the presumption of sobriety by adducing or eliciting admissible evidence to suggest, as a reasonable possibility, that he or she was intoxicated.[27] If D is able to discharge this evidential burden, a new presumption (that D was intoxicated) arises; and, if it is considered necessary to rebut this presumption, the prosecution will have to prove that D was not intoxicated.[28]

A.32   Clause 7(4) provides that if at the relevant time D was intoxicated, or is taken to have been intoxicated, then it is to be presumed that D's state of intoxication was self-induced. If D wishes to contend that his or her state of intoxication was involuntary, so as to rely on clause 2 or clause 5(3)(a), clause 7(4) goes on to provide that D must prove involuntary intoxication on the balance of probabilities.

A.33   The requirement that D must prove involuntary intoxication means that D must prove the factual basis of his or her involuntary intoxication. In the vast majority of such cases D will no doubt contend that his or her situation falls within the list of examples or cases set out in clause 6(4) and (5).

---

[25]   Clause 7(2)(a).

[26]   D may counter that he or she was sober; or perhaps contend, if intoxication is established, that he or she was involuntarily intoxicated.

[27]   Clause 7(2)(b).

[28]   Clause 7(3).

8   Consequential amendments and repeal

(1)   In section 5 of the Criminal Damage Act 1971 (c. 48) (meaning of "without lawful excuse"), in subsection (3), at the end add ", but this is subject to section 5 of the Criminal Law (Intoxication) Act 2009 (which makes provision about mistaken beliefs and intoxication)".

(2)   In section 6 of the Public Order Act 1986 (c. 64) (fault element of certain offences relating to public order), subsections (5) and (6) (which deal with the effects of intoxication) are repealed.

(3)   In section 76 of the Criminal Justice and Immigration Act 2008 (c. 4) (reasonable force for purposes of self-defence etc.), for subsection (5) substitute —

    "(5)   But —

        (a)   in relation to England and Wales, subsection (4)(b) is subject to section 5 of the Criminal Law (Intoxication) Act 2009 (which makes provision about mistaken beliefs and intoxication);

        (b)   in relation to Northern Ireland, subsection (4)(b) does not enable D to rely on any mistaken belief attributable to intoxication that was voluntarily induced."

EXPLANATORY NOTES

Clause 8

A.34   Clauses 8 sets out two amendments to and one repeal of existing legislation.

A.35   Clause 8(1) amends section 5(3) of the Criminal Damage Act 1971 to make it clear that that provision is to be read subject to clause 5.

A.36   Clause 8(2) repeals subsections (5) and (6) of section 6 of the Public Order Act 1986. These subsections are no longer necessary given the general scheme provided by this Bill.

A.37   Clause 8(3) amends section 76(5) of the Criminal Justice and Immigration Act 2008 so that (for England and Wales) reference is made to clause 5 of the Bill in cases where D relies on self-defence or the defence in section 3(1) of the Criminal Law Act 1967 and D was intoxicated.

9 Citation, commencement, application and extent

(1) This Act may be cited as the Criminal Law (Intoxication) Act 2009.

(2) This Act comes into force at the end of the period of 2 months beginning with the day on which it is passed.

(3) Nothing in this Act applies in relation to any offence committed before the Act comes into force.

(4) Nothing in this Act affects the law relating to an issue of automatism or insanity.

(5) Section 8(3), and this section, extend to England and Wales and Northern Ireland.

(6) Subject to that, this Act extends to England and Wales only.

EXPLANATORY NOTES

Clause 9

A.38   This clause is largely self-explanatory.

A.39   The only provision requiring an explanation is clause 9(4). This provides that the common law continues to govern the situation where D was intoxicated and an issue in the trial is the question whether or not D was insane (the defence of insanity) or D wishes to rely on the defence of (non-insane) automatism.

APPENDIX B
PREVIOUS RECOMMENDATIONS

THE REPORT OF THE BUTLER COMMITTEE[1]

B.1   The Committee on Mentally Abnormal Offenders dedicated a number of paragraphs of their report to the question of voluntary intoxication and criminal liability.[2] The Committee's view was that there should be no *Majewski* rule permitting a conviction for an offence of "basic intent" on the basis of self-induced intoxication if D did not have the fault element required by the definition of that offence.

B.2   In all cases D would be liable only if it could be proved that he or she acted with the culpable state of mind required for liability. If, because of evidence of self-induced intoxication, it could not be proved to the criminal standard that D acted with the required state of mind, D would not be liable for the offence charged. D would, however, be liable for a new "fall-back" offence of "dangerous intoxication" if it could be proved that, in D's state of self-induced intoxication, he or she committed the conduct element of any one of a number of "dangerous offences", such as an offence involving injury to the person.[3] The only fault the prosecution would have to prove would be that D became intoxicated voluntarily – that is to say, that D intentionally took a drug knowing that it was capable in sufficient quantity of having an intoxicating effect.[4]

B.3   If convicted of the "fall-back" offence on indictment, D would face a maximum term of one year's imprisonment if it was a first offence, and a maximum of three years' imprisonment for any subsequent conviction for the same offence.[5]

THE CRIMINAL LAW REVISION COMMITTEE'S FOURTEENTH REPORT[6]

B.4   Accepting that the harmful conduct of violent inebriates is socially unacceptable and deserving of punishment, the Criminal Law Revision Committee felt that the recommendations of the Butler Committee did not go far enough:

---

[1]   *Report of the Committee on Mentally Abnormal Offenders*, (1975) Cmnd 6244.

[2]   Above, paras 18.51 to 18.59.

[3]   Above, paras 18.54 to 18.55.

[4]   Above, paras 18.56 to 18.57.

[5]   Above, para 18.58. On summary trial the maximum suggested was six months' imprisonment.

[6]   *Offences Against the Person*, (1980) Cmnd 7844.

The record must indicate the nature of the act committed, for example whether it was an assault or a killing. It would be unfair for a defendant who has committed a relatively minor offence while voluntarily intoxicated to be labelled as having committed the same offence as a defendant who has killed. The penalty suggested is also ... insufficient to deal with serious offences such as killings or rapes while voluntarily intoxicated by drink or drugs.[7]

B.5 The majority view was, in effect, that the present common law *Majewski* rule should be codified, albeit without reference to the confusing concepts of "basic" and "specific" intent. The recommendation was that there should be a statutory provision incorporating the following test:

(1) evidence of voluntary intoxication would continue to be capable of negating the mental element in murder and the intention required for the commission of any other offence;[8]

(2) with regard to offences for which recklessness constitutes an element of the offence, if the defendant, owing to voluntary intoxication, had no appreciation of a risk which he would have appreciated had he been sober, such lack of appreciation would continue to be immaterial.[9]

B.6 According to the CLRC:

In practice juries and courts are reluctant to accept that a defendant was so drunk that he did not form any special intent which may be required or foresee any consequences of his conduct. The *Majewski* situation is rarely met but when it is the courts can, if the circumstances justify it, mitigate the penalty to such extent as is felt appropriate ...[10]

B.7 It was recognised that objections could properly be raised against the second (that is, *Majewski*) limb of the recommendation on the ground of principle, but the CLRC nevertheless concluded that codification of the common law would be less problematic than, and therefore preferable to, the creation of an additional offence.[11] The creation of a new offence, such as the offence of "doing the act while in a state of voluntary intoxication" put forward for consideration by Professors John Smith and Glanville Williams,[12] would, it was said:

---

[7] Above, para 261. The CLRC did accept, however, that the concept of voluntary intoxication should be defined in line with the recommendation of the Butler Committee.

[8] The CLRC felt that D would have a defence to a charge of rape if he was so intoxicated that he lacked the intention to have sexual intercourse (para 272).

[9] Above, para 267 (emphasis added). In formulating this test, the Committee relied on s 2.08(2) of the American Model Penal Code.

[10] Above, para 265.

[11] Above, paras 262 to 264.

[12] Above, para 263.

(1)   add to the already considerable number of matters which a jury often has to consider when deciding whether the offences charged have been proved;

(2)   give rise to difficulties in cases where one group of jurors concludes that D was drunk, but nevertheless subjectively reckless for the purposes of the offence charged, whereas the other group concludes that D was so drunk that he can be liable only for the alternative offence of "doing the act";

(3)   possibly result in defendants raising intoxication in many more trials, and seeking to plead guilty to the new offence to avoid being tried for and convicted of the offence charged, which may be regarded as the more serious offence, thereby placing the judge and prosecution in a difficult position;

(4)   give rise to confusion amongst the general public.

B.8   With regard to mistakes of fact in cases where D wishes to rely on the defence of self-defence or duress, the CLRC felt that a mistake wholly or partly induced by an intoxicant should allow D to avoid liability if the offence charged required an intention, but that it should not be permissible for D to rely on any such mistake if the offence required nothing more than recklessness.[13]

THE LAW COMMISSION'S CODIFICATION OF THE LAW – LAW COM NO 177

B.9   The CLRC's recommendations[14] were adopted in the Law Commission's Draft Criminal Code Bill,[15] in accordance with the Commission's general policy to adopt recent CLRC proposals which had not yet been acted upon by the Government.[16]

B.10   The provision in the Draft Criminal Code Bill ("clause 22") is described in the commentary as "a somewhat complex clause", the reason being that "a simpler clause on intoxication could only result from a major law reform exercise". The Law Commission concluded, however, that "like the majority of the Criminal Law Revision Committee, we are not in any case persuaded that the law as stated in clause 22 would be seriously unsatisfactory".[17]

---

[13]   Above, paras 277 to 278.

[14]   Fourteenth Report, *Offences Against the Person*, (1980) Cmnd 7844, summarised in para 279.

[15]   A Criminal Code for England and Wales: Report and Draft Criminal Code Bill (1989), Law Com No 177.

[16]   Above, Vol 1, para 3.34.

[17]   Above, Vol 2, para 8.33.

LAW COM NO 218 AND THE HOME OFFICE'S CONSULTATION PAPER

B.11 Certain aspects of clause 22 of Law Com No 177 were incorporated into clauses 21, 33 and 35 of the Commission's Draft Criminal Law Bill appended to the report Offences Against the Person and General Principles (1993), Law Com No 218. These provisions were intended to do no more than codify the existing common law rules on voluntary intoxication insofar as they were relevant to offences against the person. No attempt was made to remove any anomalies in the law.

B.12 Clause 21(1) of the Draft Criminal Law Bill provides that a person who was voluntarily intoxicated at the material time shall be treated:

    (1)   as having been aware of any risk of which he would have been aware had he not been intoxicated; and

    (2)   as not having believed in any circumstance which he would not have believed in had he not been intoxicated.

B.13 Paragraph (a) is uncontroversial and accords with clause 22(1)(a) of the Commission's Draft Criminal Code Bill.

B.14 Paragraph (b) draws no distinction between mistakes of fact as they relate to crimes of "specific intent" and mistakes of fact as they relate to allegations of recklessness.[18] This accords with the common law position as recently confirmed by the Court of Appeal in *Hatton*[19] – where it was held that D is liable for murder (a "specific intent" offence) if D killed V in the mistaken belief that V was about to launch an attack on him or her, if D's mistake arose from voluntary intoxication – but it is a departure from the Commission's Draft Criminal Code Bill.[20]

B.15 Clause 35 of the Draft Criminal Law Bill sets out definitions of intoxication and voluntary intoxication which are broadly in line with clause 22(5) to (7) of the Draft Criminal Code Bill.[21]

---

[18] See Law Com No 218, para 44.9.

[19] [2005] EWCA Crim 2951, [2006] 1 Cr App R 16 (247)

[20] See A Criminal Code for England and Wales: Report and Draft Criminal Code Bill (1989) Law Com No 177, Vol 2, para 8.42. It is to be noted that Law Com No 218 did not support the retention of this aspect of the common law. It was included in the Draft Criminal Law Bill (as cl 33(1)) pending the outcome of the Commission's project on voluntary intoxication, which was then underway, simply "to maintain the common law position on this issue ... to avoid any argument that a Bill that did not address the intoxication rules had thereby abolished them". For the Commission's final view, recommending a change in the law, see Legislating the Criminal Code: Intoxication and Criminal Liability (1995), Law Com No 229, paras 7.10 to 7.12

[21] The definition of "intoxicant" in cl 35(5) reflects the approach adopted in cl 22(5)(a) of the Draft Criminal Code Bill, save that the phrase "impair awareness or understanding" is preferred over "impair awareness or control"; the definition of "voluntary intoxication" in cl 35(2) and (3) is a refined version of cl 22(5)(b) and (c) of the Draft Criminal Code Bill; cl 35(4) repeats cl 22(6) of the Draft Criminal Code Bill; and cl 35(6) is equivalent to the evidential burden provision in cl 22(7) of the Draft Criminal Code Bill.

B.16 Finally, paragraph 13(3) of Schedule 3 to the Draft Criminal Law Bill was included to bring consistency to the law as applied to persons and property. Paragraph 13(3) would amend the "protection of property" defence in section 5(2)(b) of the Criminal Damage Act 1971 to bring it in line with the Bill's approach to self-defence in clause 27, for which (by virtue of clause 21) it would not be possible to rely on a mistaken belief of fact induced by voluntary intoxication.[22]

B.17 Following the publication of Law Com No 218 and Draft Criminal Law Bill, the Home Office published its own proposals for reforming the Offences Against the Person Act 1861 in a 1998 consultation paper.[23] The Offences Against the Person Bill appended to that paper includes a draft clause on voluntary intoxication (clause 19) which is described in the paper as "similar to that" in the Commission's Draft Criminal Law Bill. The policy of the Home Office is set out at paragraph 3.23 of the paper:

> Clause 19 sets out criteria for the courts to apply when considering whether a defendant had chosen to be drunk. There should be no loophole in the law which excuses violent behaviour simply because an attacker chose to become intoxicated and run the risks that entails.

B.18 Clause 19(1) reproduces the substance of clause 21(1) of the Commission's Draft Criminal Law Bill with some amendments to the language used.[24] It is to be noted that clause 19(1)(b) draws no distinction between mistakes of fact as they relate to crimes of "specific intent" and mistakes of fact as they relate to allegations of recklessness.

B.19 One change in the Home Office draft is that the double negative in clauses 21(1)(b) and 33(1) of the Law Commission's Draft Criminal Law Bill is removed from clause 19(1)(b) of the Home Office's Bill. Thus, a person who was voluntarily intoxicated at the material time must be treated "as having known or believed in any circumstances which he would have known or believed in had he not been intoxicated".

B.20 The double negative is a rather clumsy device, but in this context it served a useful purpose. It will usually be the case, where a defence is based on a mistaken belief, that D's intoxication led him or her mistakenly to believe that there was a circumstance which did *not* exist, for example that V was about to launch an attack, and it is that erroneous belief which he or she should *not* be permitted to rely upon. In other words, D should be regarded as not having believed that there was a non-existent circumstance (for example, that V was about to attack D) if that mistake resulted from voluntary intoxication.

---

[22] As the law stands, for the purposes of s 5(2) of the 1971 Act D is to be judged on his or her mistaken understanding of the facts even if the mistake was caused by his being voluntarily intoxicated (*Jaggard v Dickinson* [1981] QB 527). The Bill makes no amendment to s 5(2)(a) of the Act, however, as the Commission wished to consider the question as part of the (then) ongoing intoxication project.

[23] *Violence, Reforming the Offences Against the Person Act 1861*.

[24] "Must" is used instead of "shall"; and "believed" has become "known or believed".

B.21 The Commission's Draft Criminal Law Bill does not expressly provide that D should be regarded as having had a particular belief at the material time, once D's drug-induced mistaken belief has been removed from the equation (although it is implicit that D is to be regarded as having had the state of mind he or she would have had if sober). It should also be noted that the Commission's version, based on the equivalent provision in the Draft Criminal Code Bill, was intended to address the defensive situation where D made a mistake as to an exempting circumstance, particularly in relation to the defence of self-defence. The Home Office's version, by contrast, expressly attributes to D a particular state of mind and is not limited to exempting circumstances or to offences of recklessness (unlike clause 22(1)(b) of the Commission's Bill).

B.22 Finally, it is to be noted that:

(1) subsections (2), (3) and (7) of clause 19 of the Offences Against the Person Bill repeat, in effect, clause 35(1) to (3) of the Commission's Draft Criminal Law Bill (on the meaning of "voluntarily intoxicated");

(2) clause 19(4) more clearly sets out the effect of clause 35(4) of the Commission's Bill, with references to omissions as well as acts;

(3) clause 19(5) repeats the evidential burden provision in clause 35(6) of the Commission's Bill; and

(4) clause 19(6) repeats the definition of "intoxicant" in clause 35(5) of the Commission's Bill.

APPENDIX C
OTHER COMMON LAW JURISDICTIONS

INTRODUCTION

C.1 The question whether evidence of intoxication should be admissible to negative the fault element of an offence has been addressed in many other common law jurisdictions, as has the question whether there ought to be a distinction between "specific intent" and "basic intent" offences in line with the approach adopted in *DPP v Majewski* ("*Majewski*")[1] for England and Wales.

C.2 In this appendix we set out, in brief, the position for self-induced intoxication in Canada, Australia, New Zealand and the United States.

CANADA

Common law: federal jurisdiction

The distinction between "specific" and "basic" intent offences

C.3 As in England and Wales, the law in Canada draws a distinction between crimes of "basic intent" ("general intent") and "specific intent".

C.4 There have been numerous attempts by the Canadian Supreme Court to define what is meant by "specific intent" and "general intent" offences. The accepted definition is that of Fauteux J in *George*[2] (a case decided before the House of Lords' decision in *Majewski*). In that case a "general intent" offence was said to require an intent to commit the conduct element of the offence. A "specific intent" offence, on the other hand, was said to require intent as to the *purpose* in committing that act; that is, an intent as to the consequence element.[3]

C.5 The decision in *George*[4] was followed by the Supreme Court in *Bernard*.[5] In that case McIntyre J adopted the following definition of "specific" and "general" intent offences:

> The general intent offence is one in which the only intent involved relates solely to the performance of the act in question, with no further ulterior intent or purpose ... A specific intent offence is one which involves the performance of the *actus reus* coupled with an intent or purpose going beyond the mere performance of the questioned act.[6]

---

[1] [1977] AC 443.

[2] [1960] SCR 871, 877.

[3] This definition was referred to by Lord Simon in *DPP v Majewski* [1977] AC 445, 478, as "the best description of specific intent in this sense that I know".

[4] [1960] SCR 871.

[5] (1988) 67 CR (3d) 113.

[6] Above at 139.

Admissibility of evidence of self-induced intoxication

C.6   The Canadian courts have held that self-induced intoxication can be a defence to a "specific intent" offence. Evidence of intoxication will accordingly be admissible where it raises a reasonable doubt as to whether D had the "specific intent" required by the offence charged.[7]

C.7   Evidence of self-induced intoxication is inadmissible in relation to "general intent" offences (for example, rape,[8] sexual assault,[9] and assault[10]). This was established by the Supreme Court in *Leary*,[11] applying *Majewski*.

C.8   In *Daviault*,[12] however, the Supreme Court declined to follow the approach adopted in *Leary*[13] having concluded that it was incompatible with the Canadian Charter of Rights and Freedoms, which came into force in 1982. The Supreme Court considered that to exclude evidence of self-induced intoxication as a defence to "general intent" crimes, where it could be demonstrated that D was so intoxicated that it produced a state akin to insanity or automatism, was incompatible with Articles 7 and 11(d) of the Charter.[14] The Court therefore held that D would have a defence where it could be proved that he or she was so intoxicated that the "very voluntariness or consciousness of committing the act may be put into question". The legal burden would rest on D to prove on the balance of probabilities "that he was in a state of extreme intoxication that was akin to automatism or insanity" at the time of the offence.[15]

C.9   The Court's reason in *Daviault*[16] for its departure from *Leary*[17] was that D's self-induced intoxication would be causing him or her to act without the necessary elements of volition and fault. Cory J stated that to convict defendants on proof of the voluntary nature of their intoxication would be convicting them without proof of the mental element of the offence, as there was nothing to suggest that voluntary intoxication inexorably led to offending.[18]

C.10   Cory J therefore recommended a limited exception that would allow flexibility in the *Leary* rule, while conforming to the Charter's requirements:

---

[7]   *Robinson* (1996) 46 CR (4th).

[8]   *Leary* (1977) 33 CCC (2d) 473; see also *Swietlinkski* [1980] 2 SCR 956.

[9]   *Daviault* (1994) 93 CCC (3d) 21.

[10]   Above.

[11]   (1977) 33 CCC (2d) 473.

[12]   (1994) 93 CCC (3d) 21.

[13]   (1977) 33 CCC (2d) 473.

[14]   Article 7 provides for the right to life, liberty and security and the right not to be deprived thereof except in accordance with the principles of fundamental justice. Article 11 provides that any person charged with an offence has the right to be presumed innocent until proven guilty according to law.

[15]   *Daviault* (1994) 93 CCC (3d) 21, 45.

[16]   Above.

[17]   (1977) 33 CCC (2d) 473.

[18]   (1994) 93 CCC (3d) 21, 32.

This would permit evidence of extreme intoxication akin to automatism or insanity to be considered in determining whether the accused possessed the minimal mental element required for crimes of general intent.[19]

C.11 In *Daviault*,[20] the prosecution argued that a common law rule which allowed D to be acquitted in cases akin to self-induced automatism would result in a "flood" of new acquittals. Cory J rejected this argument and stated that "it [was] always open to Parliament to fashion a remedy which would make it a crime to commit a prohibited act while drunk",[21] if they felt an acquittal in such cases was unjust.

Statute: federal jurisdiction

C.12 Following the decision in *Daviault*,[22] the Canadian Parliament amended the Canadian Criminal Code. The amendments essentially re-established the position in *Leary*[23] and *Bernard*.[24]

C.13 Section 33(1) of the Canadian Criminal Code, as amended, now states that lack of intent caused by self-induced intoxication cannot be a defence to a "general intent" offence "where the accused departs markedly from [a particular] standard of care".

C.14 According to subsection (2), persons depart markedly from the stated standard of care if they are in such a state of intoxication that they are unaware of or unable to control their behaviour and "interfere or threaten to interfere with the bodily integrity of another person." Subsection (3) provides that section 33 applies in respect of an offence "that includes as an element an assault or any other interference or threat of interference by a person with the bodily integrity of another person".

C.15 This provision represented a political compromise: rolling back the practical effect of *Daviault*[25] without openly contradicting the Supreme Court on the Charter point. It therefore reinstates the pre-*Daviault* rule for "general intent" offences but restricts it to offences containing an element of assault. As the provisions of section 33 apply only to assault related "general intent" offences, *Daviault*[26] still applies to non-assault related "general intent" offences.[27]

---

[19] Above, 58.

[20] (1994) 93 CCC (3d) 21.

[21] Above, 43.

[22] (1994) 93 CCC (3d) 21.

[23] (1977) 33 CCC (2d) 473.

[24] (1988) 67 CR (3d) 113.

[25] (1994) 93 CCC (3d) 21.

[26] Above.

[27] See the discussion in Gough, "Surviving without *Majewski*" [2000] *Criminal Law Review* 719.

C.16   The Canadian Supreme Court has not yet considered whether the provisions of the Criminal Code are constitutional. The Supreme Court in British Columbia has held the provisions to be constitutional,[28] whereas the Supreme Courts of Ontario and the North West Territories have held the provisions to be unconstitutional.[29]

Summary: the position in Canada

C.17   The law in Canada may be summarised as follows:

   (1)   self-induced intoxication is relevant to "specific intent" offences to the extent that the prosecution must always prove beyond reasonable doubt that D had the "specific intent" required by the offence charged;

   (2)   self-induced intoxication is not relevant to "general intent" offences which include an element of assault;

   (3)   self-induced intoxication can be relevant to "general intent" offences which do not include an element of assault, but only if D can prove, on the balance of probabilities, "that he was in a state of extreme intoxication that was akin to automatism or insanity".

AUSTRALIA

Common law: federal jurisdiction

C.18   At common law the High Court of Australia has rejected, by a narrow majority, the rule in *Majewski* that evidence of self-induced intoxication is irrelevant in relation to a "basic intent" offence. In *O'Connor*,[30] the High Court held that evidence of self-induced intoxication is relevant if it raises a reasonable doubt as to whether D acted intentionally or voluntarily when committing the relevant act.[31] The High Court also rejected the adoption of a distinction between "specific" and "basic" intent offences, holding the distinction to be illogical.[32]

C.19   It was therefore held that self-induced intoxication could be relied upon to negative the fault element of *any* offence. Importantly, the High Court included voluntariness within its definition of the fault element of an offence, in addition to intention, knowledge and subjective recklessness. Accordingly, D cannot be held criminally responsible for an act unless it can be shown that he or she acted voluntarily with the required mental element. The High Court considered that whilst D was blameworthy for becoming intoxicated, there were no grounds for presuming that D acted voluntarily or intentionally when committing the offence charged.[33]

---

[28]   *Vickberg* (1998) 11 CR (5th) 164.

[29]   *Dunn* (1999) 28 CR (5th) 295 and *Brenton* (1999) 28 CR (5th) 308.

[30]   [1980] HCA 17; (1980-81) 146 CLR 64.

[31]   Barwick CJ, Stephen J, Murphy J and Aicken J; with Gibbs J, Mason J and Wilson J in dissent.

[32]   [1980] HCA 17, Barwick CJ at para 53, 54.

[33]   [1980] HCA 17, Barwick CJ at para 66, 67.

C.20   Defendants who deliberately became intoxicated to assist their performance of an intended act cannot, however, rely on their state of intoxication to negative the fault element of the offence charged. In such cases the intent to do the relevant act was formed before the intoxication and therefore evidence of intoxication is to be considered irrelevant.[34] Similarly those defendants who knew that they had a tendency to commit violent crimes when intoxicated are unable to rely on self-induced intoxication to negative the fault element.[35]

C.21   The majority of the High Court considered the decision in *Majewski* to have established, unacceptably, a form of liability beyond the boundaries of common law criminal responsibility. Their view was that to allow a conviction where D was voluntarily intoxicated and incapable of forming the mental element of the offence was to define a new offence. This was a role best left to Parliament, not the courts.[36]

C.22   The minority, by contrast, considered the decision in *Majewski* to be sound. Gibbs J considered the decision to be "illogical" but nevertheless satisfactory, "remembering that the common law is founded on common sense and experience rather than strict logic".[37] Mason J considered the decision in *Majewski* to accurately reflect the development of the common law, which had always held that voluntary drunkenness is not an excuse for crime.[38] His Honour felt that to abandon the rule provided for in *Majewski* would be "an exorbitant price to pay", even though the compromise was "lacking in logic".[39]

Statute: federal jurisdiction

C.23   The Commonwealth Criminal Code Act 1995 and the Criminal Code 2002 of the Australian Capital Territory (drafted in similar terms) provide that self-induced intoxication cannot "be considered in determining whether a fault element of basic intent existed".[40]

C.24   The provisions of these Codes define the fault element of "basic intent" as "a fault element of intention for a physical element that consists only of conduct".[41] A note to these provisions explains that a fault element of intention with respect to a circumstance or with respect to a result is not a fault element of "basic intent". It goes on to state that self-induced intoxication can be taken into consideration in determining whether D acted with intent, knowledge or (subjective) recklessness. In addition, section 15(5) of the Criminal Code (ACT) expressly provides that self-induced intoxication cannot be considered in assessing whether an act or omission was intended or voluntary.

---

[34]   [1980] HCA 17, Barwick CJ at para 25.

[35]   [1980] HCA 17, Stephen J at para 19.

[36]   [1980] HCA 17, Barwick CJ at para 66.

[37]   [1980] HCA 17, Gibbs J at para 6.

[38]   [1980] HCA 17, Mason J at para 3.

[39]   [1980] HCA 17, Mason J at para 15.

[40]   Section 8.2(1) of the Commonwealth Criminal Code Act 1995 and s 31(1) of the Criminal Code (2002) (ACT).

[41]   Section 8.2(2) and s 30(1).

C.25   Although self-induced intoxication cannot "be considered in determining whether a fault element of basic intent existed",[42] this does not prevent evidence of self-induced intoxication being considered in deciding whether D had a mistaken belief about facts provided D, at the material time, considered whether or not the facts existed.[43]

C.26   For offences which consist entirely of fault elements of "specific intent", if any part of a defence is based on actual knowledge or belief, evidence of intoxication may be considered in deciding whether the knowledge or belief existed. For offences consisting entirely of fault elements of "basic intent", if any part of a defence is based on actual knowledge or belief, self-induced intoxication cannot be considered in determining whether the knowledge or belief existed.[44]

New South Wales

C.27   The NSW government rejected the decision in *O'Connor*[45] by abolishing it, to remove any possible reliance on self-induced intoxication as a basis for escaping liability for certain offences.[46] The NSW government recognised the public policy considerations on which the *Majewski* decision rested, stating that to allow a defence of self-induced intoxication would be "totally unacceptable at a time when alcohol and drug abuse are such significant problems".[47]

C.28   Section 428B of the Crimes Act 1900 (NSW) lists examples of "specific intent" offences for which evidence of intoxication may be taken into account (murder is listed as such an offence, but manslaughter is not). In line with the *Majewski* decision, self-induced intoxication may be taken into account in determining whether D formed the fault element for a "specific intent" offence, but not for other offences.[48] An offence of "specific intent" is defined as an offence of which an intention to cause a specific result is an element".[49]

C.29   The Act also expressly provides that self-induced intoxication cannot be considered in determining if D committed the conduct element of the offence voluntarily.[50]

Queensland and Western Australia

C.30   Queensland and Western Australia are governed by criminal codes which contain similar provisions relating to intoxication.

---

[42]   Section 8.2(1) and s 31(1).

[43]   Section 8.1(4) and s 31(3).

[44]   Section 8.4(4) and s 33(2).

[45]   [1980] HCA 17 ; (1980-81) 146 CLR 64.

[46]   Section 428H of the Crimes Act 1900 (NSW) now provides that the common law relating to the effect of intoxication on criminal liability is abolished.

[47]   Second Reading Speech, Hansard Legislative Assembly, 6 December 1995, 4278 to 4279.

[48]   Crimes Act 1900 (NSW) , ss 428C and 428D.

[49]   Crimes Act 1900 (NSW) , ss 428B(1) and 428C(1).

[50]   Crimes Act 1900 (NSW) , s 428G.

C.31 The Criminal Code Act 1899 (QLD) provides that when an intention to cause a specific result is an element of an offence, intoxication, whether complete or partial, and whether intentional (self-induced) or unintentional (involuntary), may be taken into consideration for the purpose of ascertaining whether such an intention in fact existed.[51] The Western Australia Criminal Code 1913 is drafted in similar terms.[52]

C.32 Queensland and Western Australian courts have rejected the application of the *O'Connor* principles to the interpretation of these Codes.[53]

C.33 Offences of "basic intent" are not mentioned in the Codes. At common law, however, where the offence charged does not require proof of intention to cause a specific result, self-induced intoxication has not been allowed to negate the fault element.[54]

C.34 Furthermore, evidence of self-induced intoxication cannot be admitted to show that D's conduct was involuntary (under section 23).[55]

Tasmania

C.35 Under the Criminal Code Act 1924 (TAS), evidence of self-induced intoxication is relevant to an offence of "specific intent" in circumstances where the intoxication renders "the accused incapable of forming the specific intent".[56] According to *Snow*,[57] "specific intent" refers to the intention to bring about a specific result.

C.36 As in Queensland and Western Australia, the Code does not specify whether evidence of intoxication is admissible for offences where a "specific intent" does not form an element of the offence. The courts have, however, adopted a similar stance to those states. That is to say, evidence of self-induced intoxication cannot at common law negative the fault element of a "basic intent" offence:

> Though s 17 ... is expressly concerned only with the effect of intoxication upon crimes of specific intent and is silent as to its effect upon crimes not requiring proof of such intent, the clear implication of expressing an exculpatory exception in respect of crimes of specific intent is to exclude the possibility that intoxication could have an exculpatory effect upon other crimes.[58]

---

[51] Section 28(3).

[52] See s 28(3).

[53] See, for example, *Kusu* [1981] Qd R 136; *Cameron* (1990) 47 A Crim R 491.

[54] *Kusu* [1981] Qd R 136; *Miers* [1985] 2 QD R; *Battle* (1993) 8 WAR 449.

[55] *Bromage* [1991] 1 Qd R 1; *Battle* (1993) 8 WAR 449. Section 23 provides that a person is "not criminally responsible for an act or omission which occurs independently of the exercise of his will, or for an event which occurs by accident".

[56] Section 17(2).

[57] [1963] Tas R 271.

[58] *Palmer* [1985] Tas R 138, by Cox CJ at 155. See also *Weiderman* [1998] TASSC 12 (26 February 1998).

C.37   The Law Reform Institute of Tasmania commented negatively on the law on intoxication in 2006, principally because "the division between specific and basic intent is arbitrary and its rationale – that of acquittal for a more serious offence and conviction for a less serious offence – does not apply consistently".[59]

C.38   The report considered various options but recommended that "evidence of intoxication [should] be relevant to any mental element, including intention, knowledge (including whether the person ought to have known), foresight of the consequences, and whether the act was voluntary and intentional".[60]

Victoria

C.39   The Victorian courts continue to apply the common law principles of O'Connor.[61] No legislation has been enacted to alter this approach.

C.40   The Victorian Law Reform Commission recommended in its 1999 report[62] that the principles in O'Connor should continue to apply in Victoria. This recommendation was supported by the Victorian government.[63]

South Australia

C.41   The Criminal Consolidation Act 1935 (SA), as amended by the Criminal Law Consolidation (Intoxication) Amendment Act 1999, follows O'Connor.[64] It provides that self-induced intoxication may be taken into account if there is evidence that it caused D to act without volition, intention, knowledge or any other mental state or function relevant to criminal liability.[65]

C.42   However, the Act also includes a "fall-back" offence based on criminal negligence where D's conduct resulted in serious harm[66] but D is found not guilty of an offence by reason of his or her self-induced intoxication.[67]

Northern Territory

C.43   The Northern Territory also predominantly follows the O'Connor[68] approach.

---

[59]   Tasmanian Law Reform Institute, *Intoxication and Criminal Responsibility*, Final Report 7 (August 2006) p 8.

[60]   Above.

[61]   (1980-81) 146 CLR 64. See, for example, *R v Gill; R v Mitchell* (2005) 159 A Crim R 243; *Le Broc* [2000] VSCA 125 (28 July 2000); *R v Faure* [1999] VSCA 166 (24 September 1999).

[62]   *Inquiry into Criminal Liability for Actions Performed in a State of Self-Induced Intoxication* (1999).

[63]   Government's Response to the final report, above.

[64]   (1980-81) 146 CLR 64.

[65]   See s 268(2) and (3).

[66]   Serious mental or physical harm; or loss of, or damage to property, where the amount or value of the loss or damage exceeds $10 000 (see s 267A).

[67]   Section 268(5) provides that if D's conduct can be adjudged to have fallen short of the standard appropriate to a reasonable and sober person, D may be convicted of causing serious harm by criminal negligence. The maximum penalty for such an offence is four years' imprisonment.

C.44   Section 31 of the Criminal Code (NT) provides that D is "excused from criminal responsibility for an act, omission or event unless it was intended or foreseen by him as a possible consequence of his conduct". Section 7(1) states that regard may be had to evidence of voluntary intoxication to determine whether D is guilty or not guilty of the offence. However, it is presumed in such cases that, unless the intoxication was involuntary, D "foresaw the natural and probable consequences" of his conduct. It is for D to adduce or elicit evidence of a lack of intention or foresight on account of voluntary intoxication. If this is done, the prosecution must prove that D intended or foresaw his or her conduct.

C.45   The Code also includes an offence which ensures that voluntarily-intoxicated persons are held responsible for their actions. So, if evidence of self-induced intoxication is found to negate the fault element of the offence charged, resulting in acquittal, D may nevertheless be held criminally liable.[69]

NEW ZEALAND

C.46   The New Zealand Crimes Act 1961 contains no specific provisions on self-induced intoxication.

C.47   In the case of *Kamipeli*,[70] however, the Court of Appeal held that the distinction between "basic" and "specific" intent offences ought to be rejected. The Court considered that, whilst intoxication was not a defence to a crime, self-induced intoxication should be relevant in determining whether D had the intention or recklessness required by the offence charged.[71] It was held that whilst drunkenness should not be considered a defence in and of itself, it is further evidence which the jury must take into account.

C.48   *Kamipeli*[72] was decided before *Majewski*. In *Roulston*,[73] Woodhouse J stated that the question whether or not the *Majewski* principles applied in New Zealand remained open;[74] but the *Kamipeli* principles continue to be applied.

---

[68]   (1980-81) 146 CLR 64.

[69]   See s 154.

[70]   [1975] 2 NZLR 610.

[71]   Above, by McCarthy P at 616.

[72]   [1975] 2 NZLR 610.

[73]   (1976) 2 NZLR 644.

[74]   Above, 653 to 654.

C.49   In 1984, the New Zealand Law Reform Committee[75] endorsed the approach of the Court of Appeal in *Kamipeli*.[76] The Committee recommended that the principles established in that case should be codified so that self-induced intoxication would be relevant in determining whether D acted intentionally or recklessly. In making its recommendations, the Committee recognised public concerns relating to the acquittal of intoxicated offenders, but noted the experience of Committee members that it was in fact rare for a person to escape liability on the basis of self-induced intoxication.[77]

UNITED STATES

Common law

C.50   Although the distinction between "specific intent" and "basic intent" offences is maintained in some of the US case law,[78] it is less important than in England and Wales. The US courts instead distinguish between different types of offence to determine whether evidence of self-induced intoxication can be admitted.

C.51   For offences with a requirement of intent, and offences defined with a requirement of "knowingly" or "wilfully", if the intoxication negatives an element of the crime, D cannot be found guilty. If D was so intoxicated that he or she could not form the required intention[79] or knowledge,[80] the evidence of intoxication will be considered relevant and might provide D with a way of avoiding liability.

C.52   For offences requiring recklessness, the majority of American states accept that if the only reason why D was reckless in his or her actions is that D was too intoxicated to realise the risk he or she was taking, then D will have acted with the recklessness required by the offence.[81]

Model Penal Code

C.53   The Model Penal Code and some of the modern recodifications have adopted a similar approach to the common law. The system contained in Section 2.08(2) of the American Model Penal Code makes no reference to a distinction between "specific intent" and "basic intent" offences but provides that self-induced intoxication is of no relevance to offences including recklessness as an element. The provision states that:

> when recklessness establishes an element of the offence, if the actor, due to self-induced intoxication, is unaware of a risk of which he would have been aware had he been sober, such unawareness is immaterial.

---

[75]   Report on Intoxication as a Defence to a Criminal Charge (1984).

[76]   [1975] 2 NZLR 610.

[77]   See also "Criminal Liability for Self-Induced Intoxication" (May 1999), report of the Victorian Parliament Law Reform Committee, pp 54 to 55.

[78]   See, eg, *United States v Nacotee* 159 F.3d 1073 (7th Cir) (1998).

[79]   *Allen v United States*, 239 F.2d 172 (6th Cir) (1956).

[80]   *State v Galvin*, 147 Vt 215, 514 A.2d 705 (1986).

[81]   *State v Shine* 193 Conn 632 (1984).

C.54   American law allows D to rely on his or her mistaken belief in self-defence only if that mistake was reasonable. Accordingly, unless the mistake is one which a reasonable and sober person would have made, D cannot rely on his voluntary intoxication in support of self-defence. D is to be judged according to the standard of the reasonable sober person.[82]

Jurisdiction of the states

C.55   The rules in the United States outlined above are similar to those applied in England and Wales. There is, however, one major difference. Although most individual states allow evidence of voluntary intoxication to negate criminal liability in certain circumstances, a number of states (for example, Montana) have a wider prohibition on the admissibility of evidence of voluntary intoxication, excluding such evidence even in relation to fault requirements of intention or knowledge.

C.56   Montana's rule on intoxication was recently challenged in the United States Supreme Court.[83] Montana state law makes it clear that voluntary intoxication "may not be taken into consideration in determining the existence of a mental state." In *Montana v Egelhoff*,[84] D argued that this rule prejudiced his right to a fair trial and denied him the presumption of innocence.

C.57   A plurality of four judges found that the rule allowing for the consideration of evidence of voluntary intoxication in certain crimes was of "too recent a vintage and ha[d] not received sufficiently uniform and permanent allegiance to qualify as fundamental" and therefore a rule excluding such evidence was not unconstitutional.[85] Another judge found in favour of the state of Montana, albeit for a different reason, and the statute excluding consideration of voluntary intoxication for all crimes was therefore held to be valid. (The other four judges dissented, relying on the "simple principle [that] due process demands that D be afforded a fair opportunity to defend against the State's accusations.")

[82]   *United States v Weise* 89 F3d 502 (1996).

[83]   *Montana v Egelhoff* 518 US 37 (1996).

[84]   518 US 37 (1996).

[85]   US constitutional law states that there is no absolute right to produce evidence, but rather a due process right not to have evidence excluded when such exclusion "offends some principle of justice so rooted in the traditions and conscience of our people as to be ranked as fundamental." See *Patterson v New York* 432 US 197 (1977).

Printed in the UK for The Stationery Office Limited
on behalf of the Controller of Her Majesty's Stationery Office
ID 6011180   01/09

Printed on Paper containing 75% recycled fibre content minimum.